"What is authentic Christian pedagogy view of education that covers all of life, explains the important of learning in co.............., whole person. Our ultimate purpose in Christian education means a more radical transformation than just believing in a different worldview—rather, we are called together—heart, mind and strength—to grow as disciples of Christ."

    —JAMES DALZIEL, Dean of Education, Morling College, Australia

"Amid a wider renewal of interest in the formational dimensions of faith-informed education, Cairney brings long experience and a welcome focus on pedagogy as the whole way of life of a classroom."

    —DAVID I. SMITH, Director, Kuyers Institute for Christian Teaching and Learning, Calvin College

"Trevor Cairney has made an important and innovative contribution to Christian education in writing this book. Most importantly, he has focused on offering a practical, theologically rigorous understanding of pedagogy, which surely must be the prime, but oft-ignored, responsibility of Christian schools. In a culture that is increasingly focused on compliance and knowledge transmission, Cairney offers an inspiring, alternative vision of Christian formation."

    —TREVOR COOLING, National Institute for Christian Education Research, Canterbury Christ Church University

"A study of Trevor Cairney's book will engage you in a profound discussion with a practitioner and thinker about education. In particular you will be challenged to embrace a pedagogy which involves the shaping power of a community having as its end goal the kingdom of God. It should be read by all who want to advance the cause of education that is Christian."

    —PETER F. JENSEN, Former Archbishop of Sydney

"Trevor Cairney's book on Christian pedagogy is a highly significant contribution to one of the most important debates of our time. In a context in which Christian foundations are being dismantled at an alarming rate, it is critical that we explore how we might effectively prepare future generations to live out their faith with confidence, clarity, and compassion. There is hardly a more urgent need in our time. Cairney's emphasis on cultivation, formation, the 'transformation of habits of body and mind', on the critical role of 'the whole life of a community', and on a proper biblical emphasis on the coming kingdom of God is refreshing. How he fills all this out with careful thought that is deeply informed by a serious engagement with the teaching of the Bible lifts this to the front rank of recent books on the subject."

—MARK D. THOMPSON, Principal, Moore Theological College, Sydney

Pedagogy and Education for Life

Pedagogy and Education
FOR LIFE

A Christian Reframing of
Teaching, Learning, and Formation

Trevor H. Cairney
Foreword by Trevor A. Hart

CASCADE *Books* · Eugene, Oregon

PEDAGOGY AND EDUCATION FOR LIFE
A Christian Reframing of Teaching, Learning, and Formation

Cascade Books
An Imprint of Wipf and Stock Publishers
199 W. 8th Ave., Suite 3
Eugene, OR 97401

www.wipfandstock.com

PAPERBACK ISBN: 978-1-4982-8361-8
HARDCOVER ISBN: 978-1-4982-8363-2
EBOOK ISBN: 978-1-4982-8362-5

Cataloguing-in-Publication data:

Names: Cairney, Trevor, author. | Hart, Trevor A., foreword.

Title: Pedagogy and education for life : a Christian reframing of teaching, learning, and formation / Trevor H. Cairney ; foreword by Travor A. Hart.

Description: Eugene, OR : Cascade Books, 2018 | Includes bibliographical references and index.

Identifiers: ISBN 978-1-4982-8361-8 (paperback) | ISBN 978-1-4982-8363-2 (hardcover) | ISBN 978-1-4982-8362-5 (ebook)

Subjects: LCSH: Teaching—Religious aspects—Christianity. | Theology—Study and teaching. | Education (Christian theology).

Classification: BV4020 .C35 2018 (print) | BV4020 .C35 (ebook)

Manufactured in the U.S.A.   APRIL 24, 2018

Contents

Foreword

Is there a specifically Christian way to boil an egg? No doubt, somewhere in the wackier recesses of the internet, there is a web-page designed to persuade us that there is. Most of us, though, will continue to make choices at the breakfast table relatively unperturbed by questions concerning the fiduciary commitments of the hands preparing the food. Such commitments, we suppose, are of next to no relevance. Similarly, when I take my car to the mechanic or my teeth to the dentist, as the spanner or the high-pitched drill are about to be wielded, what I want to know is how skilled and experienced the hands wielding them are, and not whether they are baptized or unregenerate hands.

As we move up the scale from eggs, carburetors, and root canal treatments, though, and reckon with situations and professions in which the lives and well-being of whole persons (mind and soul, as well as body) are involved and implicated, questions about fiduciary commitments of one sort or another suddenly begin to impinge upon us, and to strike us as much more relevant.

There can be few contexts and professions in which the well-being of whole persons is more obviously at stake than the education of children and young adults. And, arguably, there are few areas in which the relevance, appropriateness, and nature of an explicitly religious ethos and identity are so hotly contested. In a world where the dogmas of secular humanism are able conveniently to masquerade as "neutrality" in religious terms, we are likely to be told that it is better for children to learn in an environment where questions of faith are not allowed to intrude, so as to ensure an "objective" and open-minded approach to things. What this means in practice, of course, is that the only fiduciary commitments granted unchallenged status in the public sector (escaping scrutiny, and embedded invisibly but securely in curricula) are those of secular humanism, which is anything but objective and open-minded.

In this important book Trevor Cairney, an educator of long, varied and rich experience, argues persuasively for a distinctly Christian approach to the education of the young. Education, he reminds us, is not first and foremost about successfully transmitting bodies of data or practical skills, achieving top-flight grade profiles, or churning out individuals who will be "useful" when measured by the indices of political economy. These things may all have a place (though it should be a far less exalted place than they typically enjoy in the current educational climate), but they should not be mistaken for education. Real education, the thing that above all should be permitted to shape institutions and curricula and methods, is about the formation of young lives, the cultivation of character, the enriching of body, mind, and soul through participation in communities of learning and exploring.

What makes Christian education "Christian," Cairney argues, is not the content of curricula, nor the adoption of particular pedagogical methods, but a teleology (derived from and informed by Christian faith) that orientates and motivates this learning and teaching community, the goods and goals deemed worthy of pursuit within it, worthy, indeed, of being prioritized over other possible goods and goals. It is a teleology (strictly speaking, an "eschatology") that views students in the light of a bigger and more ultimate vision than the horizons of their current intellectual accomplishments or future economic productivity, one that seeks to cultivate minds and hearts orientated not towards "employability," self-advancement or material well-being, but towards the substance of God's promise in Christ, and already beginning to bear some of its hallmarks. On such a view, it need not matter that all or even most of the students are themselves Christian, but it will matter a great deal that those into whose hands parents entrust them to be educated are. For in a real sense this is a view of teaching as a vocation every bit as "spiritual" (i.e., earthed in and sustained at every level by the presence and activity of God's Spirit) as that of those called to ordination, or to the mission field, or the religious life.

As well as a wealth of educational expertise, Cairney draws authoritatively on wide reading in theology, philosophy, sociology, psychology and numerous other disciplines in building his case. Education in its fullest sense, he suggests, is about the whole person participating in a community of learning, where desires and hopes and expectations are shaped and reshaped through imaginative and disciplined practices, and courtesy of skilled practitioners who are able to "orchestrate" and respond to the many complex forces at work not just inside but outside the classroom and the school environment.

It is a rich vision, and an inspiring one, and those with children of school age (Christian or otherwise) should hope and pray for the sorts of teachers and approaches that it calls for. Those who happen to be Christians and are, or are intending to become, teachers should read it, and then read it again, for they will find much in its pages to inspire or refresh and rejuvenate their sense of the answer to what Cairney himself identifies as the key question: not "*what* shall we teach?" or "*how* shall we teach it?", but "*why* do we teach?"

I had the privilege of delivering the New College Lectures in the University of New South Wales both in 2008 and 2015, on both occasions at Trevor's invitation as Principal of New College. The vision of education distilled in the pages of this book is one that I saw being applied and enacted among the staff and students of the College, albeit at the level of tertiary rather than primary or secondary education. It is a pleasure to have the first word in commending this work to readers by way of this foreword, though the real commendation is to be found in attending to what follows.

Trevor Hart
University of St Andrews

Acknowledgments

This book took twenty-five years to conceive, almost as many years to pluck up courage to write it, and nine years to complete. It would never have been completed without the support of many people. First among these is my wonderful and long-suffering wife, Carmen. We celebrated forty-six years of marriage together recently, and without her my life would have been sadly impoverished. We fell in love when we were both training to become teachers, we inspired and encouraged one another as we entered the teaching profession, and came to faith just two weeks apart in our early thirties. We've been blessed with two wonderful daughters (Nicole and Louise), six grandchildren (Jacob, Rebecca, Elsie, Lydia, Samuel, and Evelyne), and two godly sons-in-law (David and Jonathan). I have learned lessons from every one of these family members, including the two youngest members, Lydia (6) and Evelyne (9).

I also owe a great debt to the Board of New College, an Anglican residential college at the University of New South Wales in Sydney, where I served as Master of the College from 2002 until 2016. I was given three half blocks of sabbatical leave in my time at the college, and this allowed me to concentrate on study and writing for longer periods of time. This was invaluable. I want to give special thanks to my two chairmen at "New," Dr. Robert Doyle and Rev. Canon Bruce Morrison, for their support.

I also want to thank the many members of the editorial board of *Case Quarterly*, who served with me while Editor of this publication, and as the Director of CASE, a center for apologetics and public theology that I founded at the University of New South Wales in 2002. Working with an estimated 100-plus incredible Christian thinkers and writers while leading CASE has been a stretching experience and a great privilege. In a sense, it has been a wonderful life tutorial as I have shared and tested my ideas with so many insightful people, accepted suggestions for reading, edited their work, and listened to their ideas for research and writing.

I also owe a great debt to the wonderful scholars who responded to my invitations to present public lectures at the University over the last fifteen years. This group has included Oliver O'Donovan, Stanley Hauerwas, Jeremy Begbie, Trevor Hart, James Smith, Peter Harrison, Simon Gathercole, and John Wyatt. Having such great scholars at the college for a week at a time—with the chance to listen to them, spend time with them, and learn from them—has been a great privilege.

Finally, I wish to acknowledge a group of fellow Christians who gathered at the initiative of the then Anglican Archbishop Peter Jensen to form the Anglican Education Forum (AEF) in 2010, which he asked me to chair. This was a reading and discussion group dedicated to exploring Anglican education. We met for a day once per month. We constantly shared ideas, readings, and draft writing, for a period of almost two years. Eventually we published a book as a partial report on our deliberations. While this work interrupted my own writing, I have no doubt it enriched and enhanced my work as I engaged with and learned from this wonderful group. Special thanks go to Peter Jensen, Bryan Cowling, Michael Jensen, Claire Smith, John Collier, and Tim Wright for sharing their great wisdom and knowledge and being risk-takers.

I want to thank all of the many people who have indirectly supported me and challenged me during the writing of this book over the last nine years, including the many scholars who I cite in the book whose writing has engaged and pushed me through new doorways. I also thank Wipf & Stock for publishing the work, and for the team that has worked on the manuscript. While I accept full responsibility for any weaknesses in this publication, I am very conscious that it would have been a lesser work but for the challenge, inspiration, and support of so many people. I look forward to future conversations about the ideas within the book.

PART I

Christian Pedagogy,
Formation, and Education

Introduction:
Is There Such a Thing as Christian Pedagogy?

What normally passes for Christian education can be
more accurately named Christians educating.

—JOHN HULL[1]

The primary concern of this book is the question, "Is there such a thing as Christian pedagogy?" Others in the past have asked related questions. These have included: "Is there such a thing as a Christian curriculum?," "What does Christian education look like?," "How do we build a Christian ethos?," and so on. In the chapters that follow, I contest some of the narrowly developed definitions that have driven responses to questions such as the above. Christian teachers are often confused by Christian debates about education, and resort simply to the advice of secular theorists and experts whether educating children at school, in the church, or at home. Other writers often claim the support of Scripture to justify how they want to "do" Christian education. At times, this advice can appear to be educationally flawed.

I have two overriding criticisms of much of the work in the name of Christian education. First, it hasn't always engaged with the best secular knowledge and research while seeking to frame models of Christian education, curriculum, and pedagogy. Second, the application of the Bible to justify views on Christian education has often been decontextualized, and has demonstrated limited or poor biblical interpretation, and at times, doubtful theology.

---

1. Hull, "Aiming for Christian Education, Settling for Christians Educating," 203–23.

As I have searched the Scriptures for guidance, I have tussled with other writers on the topic. In this book, I use biblical interpretation to frame my consideration of the best secular knowledge available about teaching and human learning. This has taken me to varied fields beyond theology, including education, sociology, psychology, linguistics, semiotics, anthropology, and philosophy. In drawing on these varied fields, I have set the wisdom of other scholars against scholarship on Christian formation. The formation and education of children is spoken of in the Old Testament in books such as Proverbs and Psalms, and it is also seen in New Testament references to *paideia*, a word that has its genesis in ancient Greek philosophy and education. Greek education assumed the need to form children, not simply teach them things. Children were not seen by Greeks or Jews (nor, it would seem, early first-century Christians) as simply needing to find their own way in learning and life. Their place within varied communities of practice such as families, varied types of formal education, church, and the wider world, was given extensive guidance. Children were seen as needing to be nurtured, taught, and led into the life of communities.

The purpose of this book is not to simply revisit ancient traditions and argue for replication, but their emphasis on formation is an important part of my work. In considering formation, I do not intend to narrow my focus just to teaching, method, or curriculum. Many have done this in the past and have argued for particular Christian approaches. I want to suggest from the outset that many of these narrow approaches offer, at best, incomplete answers to the questions that matter. As such, they end up being approaches to education that while claiming to be Christian, lead to outcomes that John Hull has wisely referred to as "Christians educating." In chapter 1 I will explore the foundations of what I consider should be characteristic of Christian pedagogy and education. In later chapters I will consider what this might look like in schools, the church, and families, and of course, why?

Chapters 2 through 5 complete the first half of the book and explore the relationship of pedagogy to education, teaching, learning, community, and formation. In chapter 2, my central consideration is formation within varied communities of practice. Throughout the book, I have been driven by a central premise: education involves the whole of life of a community. I outline a definition of Christian education that has framed my work by considering biblical justification and academic scholarship across varied fields of study. Chapter 3 has a particular focus on the community and the life of the classroom and the connection of student life to the world. In particular, I consider how purpose and the goals of education have an influence on shaping all that teachers and schools do. Standpoint and *telos* are a critical part of how the education we envisage is shaped. In chapter 4, I extend the arguments in the previous chapter to consider education more holistically as embodied or enacted in classrooms and the world. In chapter 5, the final chapter in the first half of the book, I consider learning in depth and the roles that communities of practice play in the construction of meaning. To do this we consider the teacher's role within the classroom, and how the classroom life is related to meaning-making within communities.

The second half of the book shifts emphasis towards what teachers, parents, schools, and church leaders might need to do for Christian education to be more authentic and life-forming. With an emphasis on life, it addresses what might be necessary to shift our focus from success, achievement, and an emphasis on the communication and teaching of Christian ideas to a focus on formation with an orientation to the kingdom. In chapter 6 this is picked up with a challenge to adopt a different focus in relation to the varied and competing communities of practice that are the realities of life.

In chapter 7 I shift to consideration of the importance of narrative to life, and in particular to human formation. I offer a personal reflection on the role of narrative in my own story, then shift to a consideration of how God uses story and narrative in teaching to give direction to the paths of our lives. Chapter 8 is closely related to the previous chapter and considers how God has gifted humanity with the ability to imagine. The chapter considers what imagination is and how God uses it for his purposes, in forming and challenging us for the good. Finally, in chapter 9 I outline a pedagogical framework for schools and teachers as a tool to examine and evaluate the educational communities they have established, and the role the faith traditions of the school play each day in the life of the school and classroom.

1

What Is Christian Pedagogy?

Since you call on a Father who judges each person's work impartially, live out your time as foreigners here in reverent fear.

—1 PETER 1:17

This first chapter sets the stage for the development of my argument that authentic Christian pedagogy must be rooted in a clear understanding of God's purposes for his people in-between this life and the next. The Bible teaches that our lives are to be centered on knowing and honoring God in the here and now, with an eye on the future as we await Christ's return and the coming of the kingdom of God. Our true and ultimate home is not on Earth, and we are to live out our lives as "foreigners" or "aliens and strangers" (1 Pet 1:17b; 2:9–12). We live between two worlds: the current one, and the next to come. In this book, I consider what this might mean for education. A key argument in chapter 1 is that any education claiming to be Christian should be shaped by biblical wisdom and understanding. This is reflected in the definition of education that frames the book. In short:

> Education is the whole of life of a community, and the experience of its members learning to live this life, from the standpoint of a specific end goal.

The definition has two major propositions that give shape to the book. First, education is indeed about the "whole of life" of a community, not simply curriculum or method. Second, participants "learn to live this life" together from a particular standpoint. This is an education focused on the ends, rather than the means of education. The why rather than the what and how. I will argue that ends and means must always be seen in relation to the ultimate problems of life, problems that concern the nature and destiny of humankind. This should lead to a pedagogy that reflects an understanding that God made us in his image as creative, problem-solving beings, to seek him and live in relationship to him and one another. While doing this, God also called us to love, serve, and work with a knowledge of his risen Son in order to bring God glory. Education is a process of cultivation and formation. Put another way, the task of the teacher is the nurturing and transformation of habits of body and mind that enable children to fulfill God's purposes for their lives centered in Christ.

My argument for a distinctive Christian pedagogy begins with an understanding that it should encourage teachers and their children to seek the kingdom of God. This is taken up in more detail in chapter 3. With such a priority, pedagogy is shaped by different expectations, goals, and emphases. A natural tension occurs here as we seek to reconcile our views on pedagogy with school and parental goals that may reflect the desires of the world, rather than with the biblical call for our lives to be focused on the coming kingdom of God.

SEEKING "BIGGER" VIEWS OF CHRISTIAN EDUCATION AND PEDAGOGY

I want to argue in this book that on the whole, Christian parents, teachers, administrators, and clergy have too small a view of what we might generally call Christian education, and this limits the articulation of a biblically informed Christian pedagogy. By "Christian education" I mean education that is informed by Christian faith, doctrine, and theology. While the focus of this book will be on education that occurs in the context of schools, I hope what I say will also have relevance for education in the Christian home, church, and theological college. As well, I hope the book will be relevant for Christian teachers who teach in secular schools. In short, I hope my questions and answers will resonate with many of the questions others are tussling with in a variety of educational settings.

In speaking of Christian schooling, I am referring, in the first instance, to schools that claim as part of their public proclamations and statements of purpose and vision that they are founded on "Christian faith and values" (or some variation of these words). I assume—no doubt wrongly, in some cases—this means the school is founded on belief in God and acceptance of the gospel and teachings of Christ as received in the Bible.

For almost three decades I have puzzled over the question, "Is there such a thing as a distinctive and biblically mandated form of Christian education?" In the process, I have tried to reconcile my scholarship within a secular university and secular academies with my Christian faith. I have not been alone, and I have read the lucid and insightful accounts of many other fellow travelers in the past. These have included Peter Hodgson, Arthur Holmes, Stanley Hauerwas, Alasdair MacIntyre, Douglas Bloom, Mike Higton, Harry Blamires, C. John Sommerville, Mortimer Adler, James K. A. Smith, David Smith, Mark Noll, Geoff Beech, Trevor Cooling, Daniel J. Estes, and Nicholas Wolterstorff. Their work is cited within the book. These and others have helped me along the path towards my own position in relation to the question, "What is authentic Christian pedagogy?"

In 2011, I undertook to write a short book with Bryan Cowling and Michael Jensen on behalf of a group of Anglican Church leaders. The book summarized some of our thoughts at the time, while setting further direction to continue our collaborative work in our quest to identify what should be distinctive about Anglican education.[1] The book had the desired impact, promoting discussion in the wider church and leading to a major conference, as well as ongoing work within the Anglican education community.

However, this current book is a return to my own writing agenda dealing with the specific question, "What is authentic Christian pedagogy?" It brings together my thinking and research related to teaching, pedagogy, learning, and education, as well as the biblical wisdom of many, and the theological, philosophical, and historical literature of relevance to the topic. Some of the ideas had an airing at an international conference in 2012, convened by Professor Trevor Cooling, at which David Smith[2] and I were the plenary speakers.

As I indicate above, the genesis of this book spanned many years and the prompts and numerous questions thrown up by my observations of Christian education. What should motivate the Christian teacher? Will, or indeed should, my faith have an impact on or shape my teaching? What is the relationship between the Christian school and the family? The

---

1. Cairney et al., *New Perspectives in Anglican Education.*

2. Professor Trevor Cooling is the Director of the National Institute for Christian Education at Canterbury Christ Church University (UK). David Smith is Professor of Education and Professor of German at Calvin College (USA).

community? The state? What is and should be distinctive about a Christian education offered in a school that claims to be Christian? To what extent does the Bible offer insights into the specifics of education, teaching, and pedagogy? These questions were even more sharply in focus for me because I was a teacher and researcher before I became a Christian.[3]

I would be less than honest, or even foolish, not to recognize at the outset there are considerable difficulties in finding biblical guidance for many of the specific questions Christians have about education. And yet, I believe the Bible does have answers to all of life's questions. I believe first and foremost the Bible has a key story that should shape what we do in life. In the Bible, there is a central narrative tracing both the history of Judaism and Christianity, and God's redemptive plan for his people. This story matters and should give shape to the life of a Christian. In the beginning, God created . . . and it was good. But sin entered the world, man rebelled against him, and so God placed a curse upon his creation that one day would end in judgment. The Bible teaches that God always had a plan for such rebellion, a plan of redemption motivated by love, an amazing gift of grace: his own son sent to die and three days later to be raised from the dead to defeat sin and death, and one day to return to judge the living and the dead. This is a plan that provides a way for God's creation to be restored to a relationship with him. If this is the way I see Scripture's central message, my reading of its relevance for life will be shaped by this view. I opened the chapter with reference to Paul's comments in 1 Peter 1 and 2, which suggest as Christians we live a life, in a sense, in-between this life and the true life we will have with Christ. If this is reality, how should this influence education?

However, while I believe the Bible has a clear central narrative, how do we view or position our understanding of this story in relation to our life in the world? Do we see our understanding of the Bible's key story and related teachings as a means to interpret our experiences as teachers and educators? If this is the case, will our biblical understanding act as a lens primarily for critique, or as a filter to test for heresies?

Alternatively, might we see our biblical understanding and the central Christian narrative as simply sitting alongside our educational knowledge, the views of parents, national curricula, and so on? Can our knowledge of education be supported and informed by our faith and biblical knowledge?

---

3. I include my personal story of conversion and early life as part of chapter 8 that deals with narrative and story.

Another response seems to lead some to apply biblical understanding primarily in personal terms. That is, they see the Bible's teaching as transforming and shaping them as teachers and educators, while impacting how they inhabit and shape classrooms and schools. Without wanting to simply dismiss the first two approaches, my starting point as a teacher is the latter, for it is indisputable that Scripture teaches us that the gospel is about transforming lives. In Christ, we are transformed from brokenness and rebellion to a new life of wholeness and of seeking after maturity in him. As Paul teaches us in Romans 12:1–3, we are to dedicate our lives—our whole bodies—to God because of his grace and kindness to us in and through Christ. We are to seek and experience the renewing of our minds and the immediate and ongoing transformation and sanctification of our lives. We are to be reshaped as we sacrifice our lives for God's purposes.

> Therefore, I urge you, brothers, in view of God's mercy, to offer your bodies as living sacrifices, holy and pleasing to God—this is your spiritual act of worship. Do not conform any longer to the pattern of this world, but be transformed by the renewing of your mind. Then you will be able to test and approve what God's will is—his good, pleasing and perfect will. (Rom 12:1–3)

Recognizing Paul's letter to the early church in Rome and how it speaks of our faith in Christ transforming us, this book grapples with how I see this transformation as a teacher or parent impacting the way I educate children as learners, and as humans made in the image of God.[4]

As well as a central narrative, the Bible has a specific view of anthropology and what it means to be human. It speaks of the nature of family, the roles parents play, and also the way communities to some extent share responsibility for bringing up children in the ways of the Lord. The Bible has much to say on what it means to be fulfilled as a human, how God views each member of his creation, and what his priorities are for our lives. It also offers a perspective on the self and how this is actualized, and teaches us about freedom and how this impacts our roles as parents and teachers. Finally, the Bible teaches about community, each person's responsibility as members, and the role of leaders within any community, whether teacher, father, mother, prophet, and so on. How we read and understand God's word in all of these areas will change the way we act as teachers and influence our

---

4. There have been many writers who have discussed the positioning of one's theology and educational knowledge. Sara P. Little offers one helpful framework. Little, "Theology and Education," 649–51.

priorities as we shape families, classrooms, and schools. These issues will be returned to in detail in later chapters.

In summary, where we start with a task like the one I have set myself, what we bring in terms of our theology, and finally, how we see the nature of the task, will have an impact on where we end up. Hence, my aim as I approach the answering of my many questions will be to systematically work my way from first principles. My starting point for this discussion will be the defining of Christian education.

SO, WHAT IS CHRISTIAN EDUCATION?

John Hull of The Kings University College (Canada) touches on a constant unspoken observation I have made over the years. That is, what people sometimes call Christian education often lacks any distinctive markings that are recognizable across varied contexts. He writes, "What normally passes for *Christian education* can be more accurately named *Christians educating*."[5] What Hull meant by this is Christian education can end up being little more than an enhanced brand of secular education. Hull urges us that to avoid such an outcome we need to give our energies to reshaping curriculum, pedagogy, evaluation, educational goals, and school structure. This point echoes much of what I want to say in this book.

So how might we define Christian education? In framing my definition of education, I found the early work of M. V. C. Jeffreys very helpful.[6] In fact, my definition of Christian education is a modified version of one he proposed more than sixty years ago.[7] One key difference, however, is I give greater emphasis to the goal of education and the impact of the lived experiences of the members of educational communities on one another. My definition, central to this book, offers a framework for the key features of Christian education. I will elaborate on this in coming chapters. It is also foundational to what I have to say about pedagogy.

---

5. Hull, "Aiming for Christian Education," 204.

6. I am grateful to Dr. Peter Jensen for pointing me towards this book, which was a textbook when he was training to become a teacher in the 1950s.

7. Jeffreys, *Glaucon*, 3. The original definition was this: "Education is in fact nothing other than the whole of life of a community viewed from the particular standpoint of learning to live that life."

Education is the whole of life of a community, and the experience of its members learning to live this life together, from the standpoint of a specific end goal.

The definition has two major propositions I will use to frame the rest of this book. First, education is about the whole of life of a community and, second, participants learn to live this life together under the influence of a particular end goal that shapes community life. This second proposition is not clearly articulated in Jeffreys's definition, but his work does acknowledge the place of focus or standpoint. He writes, "What we believe about education implicates our beliefs about everything else. The ends and means of education must be seen in relation to the ultimate problems of life—problems that concern the nature and destiny of man."[8] What Jeffreys meant within his definition by standpoint is not completely clear, but it seems to be strongly related to what he terms "personal growth," and this he ties to "the point of view of the community," the function of which is to "conserve, transmit and renew culture."[9] This view of course would not have been unusual in the 1950s, and in some ways is not far removed from those who would urge us today that worldview, Christian values, and moral beliefs should be at the core of the teacher's concerns. However, I don't see it quite this way. While worldview, values, and moral beliefs are important and can reflect our faith, it is the end goal of our life and education itself that has the primary role in the shaping of what we do in the name of education. This is not synonymous with worldview, values, and moral beliefs.

The role of teachers and schools is to nurture, inspire, form, and influence for the good the children God gives them. Hence, the chief task of the teacher should be to create contexts for education that assist children's formation as learners, mature humans, communicators, people who work, and people who can cope in community as knowers, lovers, and desirers of God. As James Smith states, the key task of education "is the formation of our loves and desires that, in turn govern and generate action (both individual and collective)."[10] This, of course, while related, is not the same as being urged to conserve, transmit, and renew culture.

My observation of many Christian schools is they often seek to create their distinctiveness in their curriculum shaped by specific values, worldview, virtues, and so on. While we can argue a concern for these is legitimate

8. Ibid., 3.

9. Ibid., xiii.

10. James Smith, "Educating the Imagination," 9–14.

in Christian education, the focus of a transformative education should be shaped by end goals. For our means surely follow from our *telos*, that is, "the good" or aimed-for end, or goal of schooling. This is problematic, as we must not separate "means" and "ends."[11] Community values, virtues, and alternative worldviews have little impact if in conflict with one's goals. That is, they do not represent the *telos*.[12] But they must be in harmony if education is to be transformative.

Schools can easily lose sight of the goals and purpose of Christian education and become distracted by lower-level, or even conflicting priorities. Such priorities often reflect a drifting of effort and focus away from the original purpose of the schools. This is demonstrated on the home pages of many Christian schools. In his analysis of Australian Christian school websites in 2012, Bryan Cowling found some worrying inconsistencies in how key goals were articulated.[13] While many spoke of the school being founded on Christian faith and values, and some spoke of God and Christian faith, only a small number mentioned the gospel of Christ and its influence in shaping the school community and its goals. The "weight" of language and the emphasis of many was on success, lifelong learning, citizenship, tradition, academic performance, community, curriculum, standards, quality, self-esteem, heritage, culture, sport, well-being, justice, and innovation.

While these things can all be seen as good in the sight of God, they are in a sense only limited and partial indicators of—mere pointers to—a "good" Christian education. As I argued in a previous book, education involves the practice of fostering and generating in human beings ways of relating to God and the world in both word and action[14].

The central goal of Christian education should always be more ambitious than academic standards, cut-off scores, future jobs, sporting achievements, and so on. While such success is to be applauded, an authentic Christian education should be known by the character of those who graduate from it, not just success in the eyes of the world. As MacIntyre

---

11. MacIntyre, *After Virtue*, 149. MacIntyre suggests that virtues are not even a means to the end but I will come back to this and other elements of his important work later in the book.

12. Ibid., 148–49. MacIntyre draws on Aristotle's writings in the *Ethics* to suggest that "every activity, every inquiry, every practice aims at some good" and that humans have specific natures with specific aims and goals that move them toward a specific *telos*.

13. Cowling, "The Context of Anglican Education," 25–40.

14. Cairney et al., *New Perspectives in Anglican Education*, 77–88.

argues, this will be an education that leads to a "purity of heart," not just appropriate behavior and school success.[15]

The role of teachers and the school in partnership with parents is to create learning communities that work in concert with the many other communities in which all students are participants. These school communities of learners will teach and nurture and indeed form the children who God gives to us, in whatever educational context we meet them.

A major argument within this book is that for far too long, we have sought to build authentic Christian schools that end up being distracted by lower-level, or conflicting priorities. In chapter 2 I will center my discussion on the two key propositions outlined above. That is, Christian education is concerned with the whole of life of a community and, second, participants learn to live this life together under the influence of a particular standpoint that shapes community life and learning. This of course primes yet more questions. What is meant by the whole of life? What does education look like when it is seen as founded in community? And, how does such an educational community intersect with a myriad of other communities of practice—physical and virtual—that children participate in day by day?

15. MacIntyre, *After Virtue*, 203.

2

Education as Formation in Communities

Education is "embodied in the communicative life of an institution, the talk and gestures by which pupils and teachers exchange meanings even when they quarrel."

—DOUGLAS BARNES

In this chapter I will build on the discussion that was commenced in chapter 1. Having defined what I mean by pedagogy, I will discuss in detail the two key propositions within the definition, before discussing what a pedagogy might look like if we approach the task of education with an acceptance that this world is not our true home. The Bible teaches that one day Jesus will return to usher in a new age when every knee will bow before him and every tongue acknowledge him (Rom 14:11). We live in an in-between age and our pedagogy should be different as a consequence.

THE WHOLE OF LIFE OF A COMMUNITY

The Power and Impact of Day-to-Day Life

I want to suggest that in the day-to-day life of the school community children learn more than curriculum content. They learn about life and faith, beauty, loneliness, rejection, truth, humiliation, love, companionship, hate, sadness, and so on. As I have already argued in chapter 1, the thing we call education is *the whole of life of a community*, not just curriculum, teaching methods, school discipline, or even chapel and Christian studies. It seems to me that things which Christians have often worried most about have not necessarily helped create more authentic Christian classrooms and schools. Our preoccupation with curriculum, methodology, and content often reflect a desire to focus on what and how we teach, rather than why.

In the early 1980s, I was influenced by the work of English colleague Douglas Barnes, former Reader at the University of Leeds. The quote at the beginning of this chapter is from his classic book *From Communication to Curriculum*.[1] Barnes dealt at length with the fundamental importance of communication to learning and curriculum, and sought to get behind its "taken for granted" day-to-day activities. In many ways, implicit in his work was a particular pedagogy.[2] While Barnes no doubt was driven by a different *telos* than that which we might seek as Christian teachers, he saw the classroom and the school as places where minds are not simply engaged, but where curriculum and learning are experienced and enacted. Schooling can never be reduced simply to intellectual encounters designed to bring conformity to the ideas of others. Christian education is not simply about the reception of knowledge, but an engagement with the very purpose and end goal of education. That is, transformed lives as learning and life are enacted and experienced with others.

Barnes saw such enactment as involving the living out of learning as students communicated with one another in the places we call schools and classrooms.[3] Classrooms and schools are contexts in which children learn what an appropriate response is to the work of others, how they might humbly ask a question about someone else's work, how they might deal with their own (and others') success, failure, and so on. In other words, they don't simply learn the content of a curriculum or respond to the appropriate methods designed to teach; they learn about life. Barnes suggested what we do in schools is more than just teacher intentions. It is something "embodied in the communicative life of an institution, the talk and gestures by which pupils and teachers exchange meanings even when they quarrel . . ."[4]

---

1. Barnes, *From Communication to Curriculum*, 14.

2. Ibid., 14. It is important to note that Barnes did not use the word *pedagogy* but instead used the term *curriculum* in a very broad way.

3. Barnes doesn't define his use of "enactment," but it seems to be similar to Weick's usage. Weick uses the term *enactment* to recognize that the actions of people in any context are always in relationship to other people. Any individual who acts in a group such as a classroom contributes to their own self-formation and that of the group. See Weick, "Cognitive Processes in Organization," 41–74.

4. Barnes, *From Communication to Curriculum*, 14.

Yes, we can set goals and stress specific values or encourage students toward particular virtues, but we cannot do this terribly effectively if the school community fails to embody these things in the lives of the inhabitants.

Barnes's work caused me to reflect on what it is we do in schools that has an impact on the formation of our students as people, not just school learners. What Barnes did for me as an educator was lead me to consider more fully how our students' actions, as well as the activities of their minds, are influenced by education. The work of Barnes and others motivated me to look much more closely at the social and cultural dimensions of classroom life, not simply learning and teaching as intellectual and cognitive activities. I embarked on research in this area for over twenty years, in order to understand how the social and cultural practices of varied settings at home and school shaped pedagogy, and in turn children's participation and learning. But the work that has consumed me in the last decade has been a concern with how this might lead to growth in character as well as the mind. MacIntyre has been helpful in this quest, for he went even further than Barnes by challenging us to consider the need for a better understanding of the relationship between telos, education and character. In his seminal exploration of virtue and moral theory he suggests that "every activity, every inquiry, every practice aims at some good."[5]

Having reflected on these matters for almost thirty years, I have concluded that in just about every school, we think little about the communicative life of the school and probably less about the *telos*. My conclusion is if we focus our energy simply on curriculum as content or even practice, we do little to create a distinctive education leading to student formation. For it is a teacher's pedagogy, more than their curriculum or methods, that will have an influence on the formation of our students. As I introduced in chapter 1, by pedagogy I mean the way that the life of the classroom is shaped by the teacher with the participation of all others. Pedagogy cuts across or dances around the how (teaching, including method) and what (curriculum) of education. Educational pedagogy is the collective shaping of the habits, beliefs, knowledge, dispositions, actions, and words of classroom or school members, that will incline individuals and the institution toward the *telos*, or end purpose and goal of education.

In a sense, pedagogy is the embodiment (or, as Barnes would say, the enactment) of what we believe good research and our biblical understanding of personhood and God's ultimate purposes for us in Christ would

5. MacIntyre, *After Virtue*, 148.

suggest we do. Sometimes the orchestration of the life of the school community will be dominated by curriculum in the form of method, content, assessment, and so on, but always, the habits, beliefs, knowledge, dispositions, actions, and words of its members will incline them toward the *telos* or end purpose and goal of education. An authentically Christian education needs to evidence a concern for children eventually being able to imagine, desire, and embrace the kingdom of God.

Education Occurs in "Community"

The second half of my first proposition is education occurs within community. But what do I mean by a community? Jeffreys's work suggests he had a strong sense that the life of the school needed to be connected to the world outside the school:

> School and "life" are too far apart, and, what is worse, the gulf between them is accepted and taken for granted by the children, to whom it never occurs to seek any relation between school knowledge and life experience.[6]

While Jeffreys put his finger on the possible disconnectedness of the school from the world, I want to go further than he did in his work. My reading of his book suggests Jeffreys was primarily speaking of the relevance of school curriculum and learning to the practical things of life. This argument persists today and is still important, but there is much more to consider. For example, the relationship between home and school is of course the connection of two principal communities. I spent fifteen years doing research in this area,[7] and my work demonstrated that even this can be broken down much further. Categories like "home," "school," and "community" do not reflect the complexity of the multiple communities children negotiate each day. Life involves negotiating and inhabiting varied communities (as it always has), but life is arguably even more complex today. In the twenty-first century we also have multiple virtual communities to which we belong. I will talk more about this in chapters 3, 4, and 5. It is within the life of these communities that children imagine their futures and

---

6. Jeffreys, *Glaucon*, 66.

7. See, for example, Cairney and Munsie, *Beyond Tokenism*; Cairney and Ruge, *Community Literacy Practices and Schooling*; Cairney, "Beyond the Classroom Walls," 163–74; Cairney, "Community Literacy Practices and Education," 207–25.

develop hopes, desires, and a sense of the good life to which they aspire. I want to share the first of a number of vignettes in this book that I hope will ground my arguments in life and practice.

Vignette 1: Jackie Encounters Varied Communities of Practice

Jackie is a year eleven[8] student at an Australian high school. She is the eldest of three children who range in age from eleven to seventeen. She is from an average, lower-middle-class family that has a mortgage on their comfortable home, and two cars in the garage. Her mother is university-trained and is a teacher, while her father works in a government administrative clerical role. She is part of a close family with two involved parents. Neither parent is a Christian, but they have sent her to a Christian school five kilometers from their home along with her other siblings. Jackie is well-liked at school, and has a strong group of mainly non-Christian friends who share common interests in music, film, fashion, dance, and boys. Jackie is a member of multiple communities of practice:

a. Her close group of school friends.
b. The students in her art class with whom she has strong shared interests.
c. Her immediate and extended family (the latter consists of three living grandparents and cousins).
d. A dance group that she has been attending for eight years.
e. The part-time staff at the local pizza restaurant where she has worked for almost three years.
f. The members of her netball team she plays with during the summer competition.
g. A group of fellow students at a local technical college where she has been doing part-time studies in a food industry service course.
h. Her 2,500 Facebook friends and numerous other forms of social media in which she participates every day.

My reason for considering Jackie is to highlight and discuss the impact her membership in many communities might have on her life. For her,

---

8. In Australian schools, we often use "year" instead of "grade." Unless otherwise stated, when I use "year" I am speaking of the eleventh consecutive year after the first year of formal schooling, which we call "kindergarten" in my state. In other words, this is Jackie's twelfth year of formal schooling.

membership in each of the many groups in her life requires her to share specific priorities, values, and rules of engagement. Each in its own way also promotes and requires some sense of shared vision of the good life and varied practices.

James Smith's use of the term *secular liturgies* is helpful in understanding how this membership in multiple communities might impact her life. He uses the term as a synonym for worship and reminds us that the things we love and seek give meaning and direction to our lives. Any liturgy is, in Smith's words, "a pedagogy that teaches us . . . to be a certain kind of person."[9]

Even if Jackie doesn't accept the views and values of the members of each of these groups, membership requires at least tacit acceptance of, and compliance with, daily practices in order to maintain membership. Each group in its own way has an impact on Jackie's formation and her participation in the other communities of practice that make up her life. As Jackie moves in and out of these diverse communities of practice, her desires are shaped and the priorities of her life are formed. Her teachers, the school chaplain, and the Christian friends that form part of some of these communities of practice hold to views of the world that jostle for space within the mind of this teenager. If Jackie's Christian school is to have an impact on her formation, then it will do so against a backdrop of many competing stories, desires, and views of the good life. Our students are shaped in word and action as they negotiate many and varied communities of practice. James Smith, in his first New College Lecture in 2012,[10] offered his perspective on why this is so difficult:

> Christian formation and discipleship are "educational" projects in the most holistic sense: the goal isn't just to equip knowers but to form doers—which is just another way of saying that the primary target of Christian formation is the heart and the *telos* of Christian formation is love. Our doing bubbles up from our loves, whether we realize it or not. So, what's at stake in Christian formation—and Christian educational efforts rooted in that—is the formation of our loves and desires that, in turn, govern and generate action (both individual and collective).[11]

9. James Smith, *Desiring the Kingdom*, 25.

10. James Smith, "Sanctified Perception: How Worship Works."

11. James Smith, *Desiring the Kingdom*, 25, 6.

Smith reminds us, just like Barnes,[12] that students like Jackie inhabit the world as actors, not simply as spectators. Jackie moves in and out of multiple communities of practice every day. While she might be compliant and even successful within her school, this compliance might not reflect an acceptance of the view of the world her Christian teachers present to her. Our challenge within Christian schools is to move our students from being observers and compliant students, to more active learners and participants in their learning and that of others. Our pedagogy should be such that diversity of belief, desires, and views of the world are observable and discussable in supportive contexts.[13] In this way, our students can make informed choices about the things they desire, the goals for their lives, and ultimately the things they believe.

Nevertheless, school plays an important part in the formation of children as they spend a large part of their formative years living in them. As well, it is also a site for engagement and connection to many of the communities of practice they inhabit with others beyond the classroom walls.

Such formation is much more than the gaining of knowledge through school subjects; it involves learning to live the life of the multiple communities that children negotiate each day. In thinking about the place of Christian faith within this formation, James Smith has suggested that "education is nothing less than a re-narration of our identity in Christ . . . Christian education is a comprehensive project of rehabituation." Such habit formation, he suggests, is "at the intersection of stories and bodies." Education isn't just about the dissemination of information; it is more fundamentally an exercise in the formation of the whole child.[14]

A school has relationships with multiple communities beyond its boundaries. For just as a class is not completely separate from the school, so too the school can never be completely separate from the wider community. In many ways, this is even more critical for Christian schools to understand. For while many of the school's educational priorities will align closely with those of parents, community members, and government authorities, the desire to see children grow in knowledge of God, faith in Christ, and godliness in character may not.

12. Barnes, *From Communication to Curriculum.*

13. John Collier and his colleagues have spent considerable time considering how classroom dialogue in supportive contexts can help us understand the diverse backgrounds of our students. Goodlet and Collier, *Teaching Well.*

14. Smith, "Educating the Imagination," 9–14.

The Christian school needs to manage the complexities of this relationship carefully and there are many ways this might done. For example, some limit the effect by allowing only families from within Christian faith communities to attend, with the school becoming an extension of the family or church that founded the school. Others in a sense form a compact with parents and governments, and suggest they offer quality secular education, plus some religious instruction and certain requirements for Christian education and observance, if required, and if parents and students want it.

The choices each school makes have an impact on the form that education ultimately takes. But in reality, all Christian schools sit within secular and pluralistic societies, and many employ non-Christian staff, as well as Christians. They also have Christian and non-Christian families, and in almost all cases, a majority of their students have not yet owned the faith of their parents or their Christian teachers. Even in schools established by churches just for church families, the ministry is largely to a school community made up of children who have not yet reached a point of personal ascent to the Christian faith.

3 Community Practices Shape Student Engagement and the World ~claim~

Whether we like it or not, students in any school hold membership within many and varied communities, some virtual and some "in their pockets," as close as their mobile phones. All of the communities our children inhabit each day project their own priorities, values, rules of engagement, and shared vision for the good life. The impact of Facebook alone is significant and its influence cannot be underestimated, not to mention real-time communication apps like WhatsApp and Instagram that offer a continuous stream of words, images, sounds, and languages. Social media ensures constant connection to the people they choose to call their friends. I discuss the impact of such varied communities of practice in chapter 6 where I offer an insight into how Facebook changed social practices within a residential community I lead. Social media has a huge impact on school communities, extending to the way groups are formed, communication is experienced between members, the way people are included and excluded, and so on.

How each school manages its position within the world while being oriented toward the next is critical in judging the authenticity of any claim to being a Christian school. This will be seen in how a school and its teachers handle ungodly behavior, choice or censure of literature in English classes, the relationship of curriculum to popular culture, and much more. This is a key part of my discussions in chapter 7 where I explore the place of narrative in education and formation. Schools are complex social and cultural spaces where deep relationships are formed. They are not just physical places. They are social contexts where varied communities of belief and practice develop.

Etienne Wenger and Jean Lave's term "communities of practice"[15] is helpful in understanding what I am suggesting concerning membership of multiple spaces. Communities of practice are "groups of people who share a concern or a passion for something they do and learn how to do it better as they interact regularly."[16] One of the great challenges of the Christian school is to create a sense of community that is focused on eternal goals, and the implicit understanding that God made us to live our lives with a focus on the coming kingdom, not earthly kingdoms. This is exactly what David Smith and James Smith are trying to advocate in their work.[17] However, while I have found their experimental work helpful, the use of such liturgies is not, in my opinion, the primary solution for our schools, particularly at the elementary and middle school levels. I should add however, that this isn't what they are arguing. Each metacommunity,[18] such as a school, must first show evidence of a kingdom focus in the practices of its people, the priorities and goals of teachers, and the official spoken and written language of the staff. The latter of course includes how the Christian foundations of the school are explained in school websites, the many public statements by teachers concerning the relationship of faith to school policies, and the justification for rules, teaching practices, expectations, and goals. All these should be authentic, believable, and attractive. A classroom or school community should not only enable students to feel included, they should encourage members to want to be included, and to be seen as part of these communities. If our students live as observers of school or classroom

---

15. Lave and Wenger, *Situated Learning*, 98.

16. Wenger, *Communities of Practice*, 6.

17. David Smith and James Smith, *Teaching and Christian Practices*.

18. I use this term to allow me to use a term that reflects what we know as a community, that is a group of people related by common purpose, identity, and practices. At the same time, we must recognize virtually every community is made up of numerous unique but overlapping communities. Members of any metacommunity will have membership of other communities with which they might well share membership with some of the various members of a metacommunity. For example, a class, team, friendship group, work group, home room, interest group, club, and so on.

communities negotiating entry and exit each day rather than as members and participants, they will see their true place and home in other communities of practice that are more critical and seemingly relevant to them.

Building effective Christian school communities requires an understanding that schools are complex places, made up of equally complex social groupings and relationships with reflected and embedded practices. They are not just physical places, they are relational places or spaces. In effect, a patchwork of related and overlapping communities. They are essentially communities of belief and practice. I believe understanding this is foundational to the creation of authentic Christian education and pedagogy. Leading and seeking to shape metacommunities like classes or schools is what teachers and principals do every day. It requires effort to influence culture and provide direction, and it is a very difficult and complex task.

When students turn up at the school gate, they are metaphorical card-carrying members of varied communities of practice "as they come together to deal in their own fashion with the agenda of the imposing institution."[19] They inhabit multiple communities of practice in which life is shared in meaningful ways. How the school manages the interaction with, and relationships to, such diverse communities and their culture and practices is critical. Key among a range of important questions is, "Can the Christian school community help students to negotiate and learn in and from these communities, while growing in faith and their understanding of God?"

When children come to school they participate as members of varied groups, friendship cliques, families, teams, work groups, and so on, often simultaneously. They need to be eligible for membership, willing to participate, and accepted as they engage with such groups day by day. They participate socially just as much as they do intellectually.[20] This is a point to which I will return in chapter 6, but let me complete this section with a vignette from my own school-teaching experiences. I believe it illustrates the point, which I will expand on and endeavor to clarify.

Vignette 2: Chanda the "Secret" Writer

Chanda was a loud, confident, eleven-year-old African-American student who was attending an elementary school in Indiana. I was visiting her grade five class every week as part of a collaborative research project.

19. Wenger, *Communities of Practice*, 78.
20. Cairney, "The Social Foundations of Literacy," 84–96.

I would spend the day within the classroom helping the teacher to implement curriculum change. A key part of the change was to introduce a new writing program. This consisted of daily free writing on topics chosen by the students, plus other more focused pieces. We were encouraging a writers' workshop approach with regular mini-lessons,[21] individual and group conferences, publishing and sharing of writing, and so on. Chanda was our most difficult and least cooperative student. In writing lessons, she wrote nothing. And I mean nothing. Even when we placed paper in front of her and gave clear instructions to write something—"Write anything you want, Chanda"—she did not comply.

One morning as the students entered the classroom, unpacking their bags and getting prepared for the day just before the bell rang, I noticed Chanda writing something. I wandered closer and asked, "What are you doing, Chanda?"

"Nothing, Mr. Cairney."

"What is the writing?" I asked.

"Nothing, sir."

"I'd love to see your writing," I replied.

She reluctantly pushed a sheet across the table and said, "It's just music, sir, just bin writin' music."

I began to read her quite poetic and rhythmical writing, and discovered that there were a dozen or more examples like the first that I picked up. Yes, it was music! Chanda went on to share that she had been writing music at home for some time and it was one of her passions.

What I discovered that day was while Chanda saw no point and little meaning in doing what she saw as school writing, she loved writing at home. And she wrote for other readers who were part of a different community of learners—some within the class, others in the wider school community, and some from her friendship groups outside school. And of course they all participated in this community of practice that had little relationship to her school classroom and teacher. Interestingly, the idea of trying to make pedagogy and classroom practice more culturally relevant is not a new idea. Gloria Ladson-Billings, for example, has argued for over twenty years that we need to embrace "a pedagogy that empowers students intellectually, socially, emotionally, and politically by using cultural referents to impart

---

21. See Atwell, *In the Middle*. This book provides a good introduction to workshop-based approaches to writing.

knowledge, skills, and attitudes."[22] In fact, there are many examples within the field where teachers and researchers are embracing what some have called a "hip-hop pedagogy."[23]

What this vignette illustrates is many of the communities of practice that children participate in are not under our control within schools, nor do we have membership in them. As well, there is often a mismatch between what is valued in some of the significant communities of practice our students inhabit, and those within the school. This is an important point I will return to later in the chapter. I will also discuss the reality that in the present age many of these communities are as much virtual communities as physical communities, tied together by a complex fabric of social media.

𝒷 LEARNING TO LIVE THAT LIFE

The second proposition derived from my definition of education is that participants in schooling learn to live their lives together at school from a particular standpoint or point of view. That is, a shared understanding that is born of life together within community and that is focused on a specific end goal, which, as James Smith reminds us, shapes "desire." I will discuss this in more detail in chapter 3.[24]

The task of Christian teachers is to orient their students and the life of school communities of practice to the kingdom of God! We will do this as teachers who hopefully understand that our lives, not just our words and the curriculum, will help children imagine this kingdom, desire it, and seek after the good it promises. In a sense, we become teaching apologists pointing our students toward Christ. As David Hohne reminds us,[25] an apologetic person is one whose life and words commend the God they trust in. The Apostle Peter implores the church:

> Live such good lives among the pagans that, though they accuse you of doing wrong, they may see your good deeds and glorify God on the day he visits us." (1 Pet 2:12)

The Christian school is to be a community that is, in a sense, its own apologetic for Christ. Its members, and the school community life as a

---

22. Ladson-Billings, *The Dreamkeepers*, 17–18.

23. See, for example, Banks, "Hip Hop as Pedagogy," 243–59.

24. James Smith, *Desiring the Kingdom*, 39–40.

25. Hohne, "Becoming an Apologetic Person," 4.

whole, should suggest there is something different about this gathering of people. As James Smith reminds us, there must be a focus on the kingdom of God, not on earthly kingdoms and desires.[26] Smith argues the goal of Christian worship and Christian education should be to "sanctify perception" in order to shape us as Christians and mold our habitual dispositions. Too easily individuals—and indeed institutions—become habituated to ways of life that run counter to what God envisions for their flourishing. Smith suggests the vehicle for this is a form of unconscious liturgical formation constantly at work, into which we are "unwittingly conscripted into stories that are rival tellings of what's in store for the world." These narratives and their metaphorical power "seep into our bones" in such a way that they come to dominate our background and thus begin to shape our very perception of the world. This in turn orients our habitual action.[27]

Similarly, Bernard Meland suggests the ultimate goal of education is not technical information, useful practices, or specific moral values, but a search for a "higher goodness." Rather, we need to provide space for developing our students in other ways that are also reflective, imaginative, and spiritual.[28]

God made us with an inner desire to seek the one who made us. As Ecclesiastes 3:11 reminds us,

> He has made everything beautiful in its time. He has also set eternity in the human heart; yet no one can fathom what God has done from beginning to end.

But at the same time, sin pushes us in a different direction. There is great inner confusion of the heart. Our students develop different loves that offer alternative purposes and desires which can shake and shift their allegiance to the kingdom of God. Through a complex repertoire of secular liturgies "we are assimilated to the earthly city or disordered loves, governed by self-love."[29] Often this is communicated through the stories we tell and those that are privileged in our classrooms and the school in general. Such stories are an important pointer to the hoped-for life that we suggest schooling will enable.[30] The Christian school's task is to ensure the orches-

26. James K. A. Smith presented two lectures on the theme "Imagining the Kingdom: On Christian Discipleship and Action," May 23–24, 2012.

27. James Smith, *Desiring the Kingdom*, 52–55.

28. Meland, *Higher Education and the Human Spirit*, 5–6.

29. James Smith, "Imagining the Kingdom," 140–41.

30. Cairney, "Storytelling and Life," 3–8.

tra of life at school is not a random cacophony of unrelated noises, but the presentation of an alternative *telos* that will shape character and lives. I will return to this theme again in chapter 6 and in chapter 8, where I will also consider the place of the imagination.

In summary, the education offered in Christian schools is situated in the whole of life in the school, and this in turn is situated within the child's complete life that transcends varied and multiple communities of practice, both real and virtual. Students inhabit many communities of practice simultaneously, in the class, the playground, and outside the school, virtually as well as physically. What is offered in the name of education is read by students within their schools, but then reread within other communities, as it is interpreted as part of the daily activities and rituals of schooling. This is the great challenge we face and which is explored in the rest of this book.

3

Standpoint, Pedagogy, and Formation

In the past, people received their basic orientation from the family, school, and church. In the present media culture, however, images and celebrities are "replacing families, schools, and churches as arbiters of taste, value, and thought."

—KEVIN VANHOOZER[1]

I ended the last chapter with the comment that education offered in Christian schools needs to be situated in the whole of life. In this chapter I want to explore what this might look like by looking at standpoint, the last part of the definition of education that has shaped the book. While it is easy to describe the complexity of the world that teachers and their students face each day, how do we help our students negotiate their way through it in the hope they might find the only destination that offers eternal rewards? Furthermore, how do we create environments in which children live and are connected to the school, while at the same time growing and learning in ways that focus their lives and imaginations on the kingdom of God? How do we shape the whole of life of a community viewed from the standpoint of the kingdom of God for the good of all who attend our schools?

1. Vanhoozer, "What is Everyday Theology?," 29.

A *TELOS* THAT WILL TRANSFORM OUR PEDAGOGY AND OUR STUDENTS

What we do as teachers is meant to help the children we teach take their place as grown humans and mature citizens in the family of God. If our ultimate purpose is to know God, it matters how we teach, how we encourage learning, the nature of the social structures we promote, and so on. If we keep our sights fixed on the goal of seeing all children knowing, accepting, and following Christ, then what we do matters a great deal. But does it matter how we teach? In one sense, the answer is no for research suggests there is no one best approach to teaching, no limited set of ideal methods of instruction.[2] But as I have said a number of times, my claim in this book is while there might be varied methods we can use as teachers, the Bible gives us a clear purpose. Christian education is to be kingdom-focused, and if so, it must communicate the intended end goal of this education. This will be a *telos* that is centered on the kingdom of God, not simply earthly success and achievement. There is a relationship between our priorities shaped by the gospel, our faith in Christ, how we live out and speak of this faith, and our actions (Phil 1:27; Jas 2:14–26). The things we teach and the way we do it cannot be separated from the life of the school community, nor for that matter communities outside the school. Our pedagogical practices will lead to the creation of a classroom life that has the potential to speak to our students about what is important in the world of the classroom, and consequently, what matters in the world.

Central to this of course is conversation and human interaction as we live and learn. This is what we discussed in chapter 2 when we explored Douglas Barnes and his suggestion that education is "embodied in the communicative life of an institution."[3] Similarly, this is also what Trevor Cooling and David Smith are speaking of with the "what if" approach to learning.[4]

---

2. The debate about what methods are best to teach children has raged for centuries. In the last century there has been heated debate and conflicting research evidence about overall approaches to learning (e.g., direct instruction versus discovery learning) as well as in relation to specific curriculum areas. Perhaps literacy has created the greatest debate, with teachers and researchers debating the relative merits of skills-based phonics approaches verses whole-word or meaning-based approaches. The reality is most methods can work when appropriate for the particular needs of the learner and when in the hands of a committed and well-trained teacher.

3. Barnes, *From Communication to Curriculum*, 14.

4. This is an approach to learning in Christian schools. More information can be found at http://www.whatiflearning.com/information. The key architects of this work

A key difference however is that unlike Barnes, Cooling is starting with an awareness that faith should impact how we see the world. It should also impact how we develop learning strategies that encourage interaction and engagement. Finally, Cooling argues we should reshape practice to fit with the Christian aspirations teachers have for their students.[5]

As Arthur Holmes reminds us, from ancient times we have been aware that we learn with others. Indeed, the rhetorical tradition of Socrates, which has influenced Holme's work, recognized that we learn best with others. While this rhetorical tradition was much more a case of the young sitting at the feet of the teacher, nonetheless at the base of this approach was the understanding that we are formed as we wrestle with ideas and the world with others. And of course, Holmes reminds us that while we might interact and learn together, Augustine's *Confessions* were founded on an understanding that

> every good he experiences and all truth he learns come ultimately from God and are occasions for praise. God is the being "by whom all things are true that are true, and all things are good that are good."[6]

PEDAGOGY'S RELATIONSHIP TO FORMATION

Any discussion of pedagogy is complicated today because the term has been used and abused in many ways. It is commonly used as an adjective rather than as a verb. It has been captured by numerous interest groups.[7] However, if we look carefully at its etymology, we will find the word is as old as formal education itself. It was derived from the Greek *paidagogeo*, a compound of *paidos* (child), and *agogos* (one who leads or guides). For the Ancient Greeks, its purpose was to lead the child as they grew in body, mind, and spirit. It involved "an interaction between one who acts and one who is acted upon."[8] Children were not assumed to find their own way into the community through a process of osmosis or discovery, but were lead

were Trevor Cooling, David Smith and Margaret Cooling.

5. Cooling et al., *Christian Faith in English Church Schools,* 5.

6. Holmes, *Building the Christian Academy,* 26.

7. I will comment later in the chapter on the way pedagogy has been taken captive by critical theorists, feminists, and other groups with agendas of their own that involve shaping the character of our children.

8. Gurley, "Platonic *Paideia*," 351–77.

into it. It was also much more than teaching content, specific subjects, and skills. The term as the ancient Greeks understood it gave rise to the word *paideia*, which for first-century Greeks meant the passage from boyhood to manhood, a process of becoming fully human, or of turning young men into citizens.[9]

The intent of *paideia* was to create a specific kind of Greek citizen who could take their place in Greek society as a leader. The ancient teacher had in focus a moral end, not a technocratic one. The word *paideia* is what Paul uses in Ephesians 6:4. It is often translated as "discipline," which for the Greeks and Paul meant "bring[ing] them up in the discipline and instruction of the Lord." For Paul, who was taught by leading scholars in the Greek tradition, it was a form of education that he not only understood, but was the way he was taught, probably from the age of five years as was the custom in families of privilege.

The emphasis on formation is critical to the model of pedagogy advocated in this book. It is a pedagogy that reflects and is interwoven into the daily life of any community, a pedagogy that will see their classes, schools, and students transformed, for the Bible's central message is about our transformation in and through Christ. We are what we live, not just what content is learned, the worldview the teacher holds, the exams sat, assignments completed, and so on. It is within the life of the community that lives and character are shaped.

In effect, pedagogy, as I am defining it, is a term that attempts to encompass the essence of how teachers orchestrate and sustain classroom learning and life, and of course it is driven by an intent and *telos*. This orchestration in the Christian school should always be approached with the formation of the child for the glory of God as the priority. To consider a teacher's pedagogy, we also need to consider the teacher's knowledge, beliefs, and goals that shape their actions.[10]

In a sense, pedagogy is the embodiment (or Barnes would say, the enactment) of what good research, sound biblical understanding of personhood, and God's ultimate purposes for us in Christ would suggest we

---

9. One of the best introductions to *paideia* can be found in Hodgson, *God's Wisdom*.

10. Beech, *Christians as Teachers*, 115–46. Beech has an interesting discussion in his book concerning the way teacher beliefs can have an impact on even the most mundane of tasks in the classroom. He suggests teaching Christianly means all activities can have pedagogical significance. While I'm not prepared to go as far as Beech does in embracing worldview as the shaper of how we experience all things, I do share his belief that why we teach is more important than what it is.

should do. It is about how we shape classroom communities that help our children learn as they live different lives within the school community and beyond. Our aim should be to help them see how they can live their lives across the numerous communities of practice that constitute their world, and yet still grow in Christ.

Pedagogy, I want to suggest, determines our focus and enables us to place our mark on children in ways that truly differentiate our schools from secular schools. Not completely, for Christians will work in those places and Christian families will be part of them too. If our schools end up completely alienated from the world, how can our students then make their way in the world? As well, God will be at work in non-Christian families who like us are made in the image of God, and there will be "common grace" and "general revelation" at work[11].

In some sense, pedagogy is the what, how, and the why of teaching, all rolled together. One thing worth noting is the why does not really change,[12] but the what and how can. Sometimes our orchestration of the life of the school community will be dominated by one more than the other. But always, our habits, beliefs, knowledge, dispositions, actions, and words are, in essence, the key components of pedagogy, and they incline us toward the *telos* specified as the good. But our pedagogy doesn't sit outside curriculum, or a teacher's monitoring behavior, as they veto good and bad practices, or ideas that don't fit within one's worldview or values. Rather, it encapsulates all we do in the classroom to create and sustain a community, one focused on a coming kingdom. For you see, if it is an authentic Christian education—in all we do, say, sanction, and plan—it should be centered on the end goal of seeing young people growing as people who one day will be a part of the family of God. Our pedagogy needs to intersect with our desire to see children embrace the kingdom of God.

We all know that excellent teachers make a difference to children, but do you ever wonder what makes a great teacher?[13] Ask some students or

---

11. "Special revelation" is the self-revelation of God in the Scriptures, seen most clearly in the gospel of Christ. "General revelation" is God's self-revelation seen throughout creation, including the activities of humanity in places like schools.

12. This comment assumes the purposes of education are the key and that answers to why-type questions like "why teach fractions?," relate to curriculum goals and justification, not higher-order why questions that have eternal consequences.

13. I was part of a national research team that selected a number of teachers judged to be outstanding based on the extent to which students in their classes improved on national testing. This was controlled for the starting standard of all students and in effect

their parents. Educational research evidence for decades has been suggesting if a child has one good teacher in their lifetime (memorable, inspiring, respected, compassionate, and so on) it can have whole-of-life significance. By the grace of God (his common grace in action) some of these teachers may not be Christians. When you ask people to share the names of great teachers, the reasons for their greatness are very diverse, but the great Christian teacher will be known by more than their ability to impart knowledge. They will be teachers who seem to know their students, who have a deep commitment to you, and who cope with your failures and celebrate your successes. They will have demonstrated patience with your frailties, yet a willingness to correct and point you in other directions when necessary.

Vignette 3: Inta and Integrated Learning

Part I

I team-taught with a woman in a country town many years ago in a class for five-year-olds in their first year at school. I was present as a researcher, participating fully in the life of the classroom. While my role was to observe and record what I saw, collect artifacts, and so on, I was very much a teacher as well. There were many things that impressed me about Inta, but several stood out.

First, she had an excellent knowledge of curriculum and had been teaching for thirty years, mainly with very young children aged five to six and in their first year of formal schooling. Second, she used a variety of strategies to engage her students. These included drill, repetition, creative exploration, self-directed learning, imaginative exploration, directed discussions, written work, and use of varied means of expression (e.g., writing, speaking, drawing, drama, practical and creative activities). Third, she was constantly observing behavior, not just to control it, but to monitor learning and the personal participation of all students in the classroom (and even the playground). Fourth, she engaged with every child in multiple ways every day, in groups, as a class, one-to-one, through observation, questioning, correcting behavior, marking work, making suggestions, and

---

was a measure of value adding. The teachers chosen had many personal qualities that set them apart, and a major part of what made them so good was reflected in their personal pedagogy. See Louden, et al. *In Teachers' Hands*, 178–83. Additional information can be obtained here: http://research.acer.edu.au/cgi/viewcontent.cgi?article=1001&context=m onitoring_learning.

so on. Finally, she was constantly monitoring the well-being, happiness, focus, and participation of every child.

As I reflected on the data I was collecting, I asked myself what made Inta such a great teacher, it became obvious from my field notes that it was her purpose and her sense of what mattered most for these children. What was good about her as a teacher, in contrast to what is sometimes wrong with some other teachers, was her focus and intent, and the higher-level goals that gave direction to her work.

What was also obvious was she used her knowledge to excite the class, to monitor progress, and to encourage learning. These are three of the key things that marked her actions as a fine teacher:

a. She observed to monitor progress in learning, but also to track personal development and growth, not just to correct and discipline inappropriate behavior.
b. She used a variety of teaching and learning strategies, not as a counter to boredom and to reduce discipline problems, but to engage all learners in varied ways that suited their learning styles.
c. She spoke to and rebuked her students when necessary to direct them toward higher purposes like learning, but also towards patience, self-control, love, kindness, and an interest in how God was at work in their lives. Her constant monitoring supported the twin goals of learning and also their growth spiritually and emotionally.

It was her pedagogy that set Inta apart. The way she orchestrated and sustained classroom learning and life was done with the formation of the child for the glory of God as her priority. This was evident in classroom life. Pedagogy requires more than just content; in fact Inta's higher purpose could be achieved with different content and classroom strategies. To consider a teacher's pedagogy, we need to consider the teacher's knowledge, beliefs, and goals that shape their actions.

It is our pedagogy that ultimately gives shape to the very nature, climate, and culture of a classroom or school. Pedagogy is vital to the creation of communities of practice that are consistent with the wisdom and purposes of God. We will find few Christian distinctives in methods, curriculum, or content, but hopefully many things in a teacher's pedagogy that we can observe as wise practices consistent with our Maker's purposes and specifications. It is pedagogy that shapes the learning communities teachers create, whether deliberately or unknowingly, and which ultimately is critical in the formation of the child.

In summation, pedagogy is revealed in our words, actions, priorities, and beliefs. Ultimately, it reflects what we see as the purpose of our life, the lives of our children, and the role education plays in these goals. Our pedagogy should mirror the *telos*, the end goal of the education we offer children. All we are and do should point to this end goal or purpose.

HAVING A PARTICULAR STANDPOINT THAT SHAPES PRACTICE

As my initial definition indicates, education is "the whole of life of a community," not just the curriculum, the methodological skills of the teacher, or the worldview the school promotes. Authentic Christian communities have an essence or culture that is shaped by a common faith and a shared *telos*. That is, its members begin to accept a common standpoint and end goal in life.

M. V. C. Jeffreys's writing on education that influenced my definition of education placed great importance on the values that derive from a view of the world shaped by an understanding of the Christian gospel, and a strong incarnational view of existence. He reminded us that history and humanity's existence are both "transcendent" and "immanent." His incarnational view of the world centered on an understanding of biblical history and the person of Christ. The outcome in Jeffreys's view of such a standpoint is a right view of humanity and our purpose. He also saw it as offering a moral framework and values that allow us to judge right and wrong, beauty and ugliness, the honorable and dishonorable, good and evil, and so on. This, he believed, links to the "aims" of education and must be the basis and foundation of any Christian education. He suggested that "education in liberal democracies is distressingly nebulous in its aims."[14]

One of the problems with the word standpoint is it is broad and can be used in varied ways. However, for Jeffreys a standpoint is a reference point. What is the reference point from which you make sense of your world, respond to it, and live a life of faith? Jeffreys's views are very much founded on an incarnational view of Christ, but how does this shape classroom and school life? In part, Jeffreys saw standpoint as centered on belief that also had associated values, but standpoint must be more than this, for if it is just

14. Jeffreys, *Glaucon*, 61.

about values, we will end up spending much time on their articulation, and attempts to teach and transmit them. With such an approach, there is little guarantee we can influence the standpoints of our students. His arguments against a simple didactic values framework are also relevent in relation to worldview theory. Here, a system of beliefs, ideas, and doctrines are seen as needing to give shape to the Christian response to the world and how we live within it. An understanding of worldview, and the acceptance of an appropriate worldview, is seen as critical for the Christian teacher and the Christian school. When taken to extremes, ideas are seen as driving what we do, how we respond, how we deal with the circumstances of life as teachers, and so on. However, like James Smith, I caution against this approach. He argues that placing worldview at the center of Christian education has the tendency to reduce how we understand and pass on our faith to a process that is bound by "ideas, principles, claims, and propositions that are known and believed."[15]

Values frameworks and worldview theory, like any standpoint based on presuppositions, while relevant, can potentially limit the impact of Christian education on some children. I want to suggest that neither values nor worldview theory gives us the right standpoint from which to view life and create an authentic and distinctive pedagogical framework for Christian education. I say this because while I believe both contribute much to what is good about teaching, they do not necessarily do much to offer our students an alternative view of the good life. Both often fail to sufficiently connect with the lives our students live as they move in and out of varied and complex communities of practice.

Of course, more worrying are the numerous secular versions of pedagogy that are proposed. Like many words with ancient roots, pedagogy has been taken captive by secular academics, and some who bring varied theologies (e.g., liberation theology). At the heart of much of this work is a desire to use education as a vehicle for freedom from perceived bondage to the natural and social world. This has led some to advocate a pedagogy promoting choice, openness to the views of others and opposition to injustice of all kinds. This movement is centered on consciousness-raising so individuals can take greater control of their learning and their futures. Paulo Freire, for example, realized long before I did that for significant social change to occur in people and societies, you need to change hearts as well as minds. Freire, of course, has been very influential in education, and his writing has

---

15. James Smith, *Desiring the Kingdom*, 32.

in effect led to the development of a form of secular leftist liturgy that has a different and narrower *telos* in mind, namely, social transformation.[16] My goal is more ambitious than this; I want Christian schools to see their end goal as faith in God, and a desire to serve him in seeking the fulfillment of his kingdom. If this is the case, social transformation would of course also be a consequence, as believers seek to live in ways that honor God. Strangely, in one sense, alternative views of pedagogy are more committed to human formation than some Christian schools, for while they might be seeking freedom from various faith traditions, the Bible teaches us they are exchanging a life as a disciple of God's Son for bondage to something else.

Tim Keller writes in *The Reason for God* that

> freedom can't be simply defined in negative terms as the absence of confinement and constraint. In fact, in many cases. Confinement and constraint is actually a means to liberation.[17]

What Keller is reminding us is there is no such thing as spiritual neutrality. When God rescues us from an alternative philosophy, belief, or worldview, you don't become a stateless person, a citizen of nothing, an autonomous individual who belongs nowhere. When God takes hold of your life he makes you a citizen of the kingdom of Christ. Paul makes this clear in his letter to the Romans. He writes in Romans 6 that when one accepts the Christian faith you change from one master of your destiny to another:

> But thanks be to God that, though you used to be slaves to sin, you have come to obey from your heart the pattern of teaching that has now claimed your allegiance. You have been set free from sin and have become slaves to righteousness. (Rom 6:17–18)

Christian schools must be concerned about how they can recapture the term pedagogy for its right use. When I urge readers to seek right pedagogy, I mean no less than a pedagogy informed by the best of educational wisdom and research and our faith and knowledge of God, a pedagogy informed by the Scriptures and given to us by the power of the Spirit, a gift of grace. This should lead to a framework that will reflect God's purposes for us, and ultimately focus hearts and minds towards his kingdom. I have spent considerable time developing just such a framework and will discuss it in more detail in chapter 9.

---

16. Freire, *Pedagogy of the Oppressed*.

17. Keller, *The Reason for God*, 45.

IN SEARCH OF A CHRISTIAN EDUCATION SITUATED
BETWEEN TWO WORLDS

One of the great challenges for Christian educators is education is very much focused on success in this world, an earthly citizenship. But as the Apostle Peter reminded us, we are to "live [our] lives as strangers here in reverent fear" (1 Pet 3:17b). At times our Christian schools can seem well removed from this sense of being shaped by this imperative. Many schools seem to fall into one of two major errors. Some seem to embrace priorities, goals, and practices that are focused on worldly success, wealth, and excellence, while others seem to separate themselves and become strange enclaves set against the world. One extreme embraces the aims, ideals, and loves of the prevailing culture, while the other seeks to build walls and escape from a secular society in which they perceive little of the work of God. Both are misguided. The latter is always well-intentioned and is defended using Scripture. But it often fails to understand that while we are not "of this world," we all must live in it and understand that God is at work in the cultural practices of its people.

Kevin Vanhoozer reminds us of the four key doctrines that support such a view of the world. First, the incarnation reminds us God is always at work in his world to make himself known. Second, general revelation suggests some knowledge of God is available to all through his creation. Third, there is common grace as the presence of good can be seen in many people, events, and practices. Fourth, the *imago Dei*, God's image, can be seen in the activities of humanity in ruling, filling, working, and keeping his world. If we accept this, then to be in the image of God means we are all "culture makers."[18]

Simply reading the world through the Bible—"our spectacles of faith," as Calvin described it—is not the same as living in the world.[19] Our task within Christian schools—as for Christians in their daily walk—is to help children come to an understanding and acceptance of the Christian faith, and to live their lives while negotiating the world of which they are a part. Our schools should be places that are shaped by sound everyday theology as children and teachers read the world and act on it, as well as in it. Classroom life has many impacts on our children; some are obvious, but others almost work invisibly. Much is learned in and through the web of

18. Vanhoozer, "What is Everyday Theology?," 42–43.

19. Ibid., 41.

relationships that connect the at times disparate experiences within the life of any classroom and school.

LEARNING TAKES PLACE WITHIN A WEB OF RELATIONSHIPS

As I have already pointed out earlier in the chapter, classroom and school life consist of a complex web of social relationships amongst people. This includes relationships between teachers and students, parents and teachers, and amongst students themselves. Students also have membership in groups or communities of practice that require members to build relationships with one another. Many of these relationships can be invisible to the teacher.

As participants in schooling, they engage and interact with one another, and develop rules (both explicit and implicit) for group life. They also identify what counts as appropriate behavior and language, and what is valued and gives the members of groups status. Group members also develop ways of seeing the world, values, goods that have significance, and so on. All of this operates to some extent within the boundaries of what we see as curriculum, but it also operates in parallel with, and sometimes even in opposition to, the mandated curriculum.[20] Let me share a vignette illustrating a classroom example where we can see this operating positively while remaining consistent with mandated curriculum.

Vignette 4: Inta and the Power of Classroom Relationships

Part II

This vignette relates to the same classroom and teacher featured earlier in the chapter. It was recorded by me as a participant observer as part of the same research project. The teacher again was Inta.[21] On my first day I observed a boy named Brock eagerly writing in a "magic cave" constructed as a retreat area by the teacher. I stopped to ask how he came up with his idea for a story about people visiting strange lands at the top of a tree. He

20. I am using the term *curriculum* in the narrower sense here of what we teach and the methods we use to teach the content.

21. Cairney, *Pathways to Literacy*, 23–29.

replied, "Well, it was like Chlorissa. That book [*The Enchanted Wood*] had children who moved to the country. I changed it around."

Brock's piece based on the *The Enchanted Wood*[22] was primed (at least in part) by the fact that Chlorissa had done this earlier. Similarly, Kylie, who wrote a poetry book titled "A Rocket in my Pocket," decided to pursue this writing as a response to an exchange with a friend. I asked her, "So, why did you write a poem today?"

"Because my partner said I could write a poem—we're going to make a book."

"Where did you get the idea from?"

"Because we need a story about it."

"Who had the idea first?"

"I don't know, it was probably Brock who said it."

Kylie and Brock's use of prior texts was influenced and shaped by the relationships between participants in this literary environment. Kylie felt almost compelled to do what Brock gave her permission to do. While they were part of the same classroom, they made choices as learners as part of a complex web of relationships, all of which exerted influence on the choices they made, the things that were valued, and the enactment of curriculum. There was also an intertextual connection with the Dr. Seuss book of poetry *There's a Wocket in My Pocket*.[23]

In my time in Inta's classroom I identified ten "Blyton-type" stories.[24] The first major piece of writing was produced by Amanda (age five) during a single week in March. This piece was titled "The Enchanted Wood"[25] and was a retelling of the first two chapters of Blyton's book of the same name. It was typed by an aide and published for other readers within the class. While Amanda and Sally's stories were the first major pieces, there had been a number of smaller pieces of writing that referred to The Faraway Tree books, as well as additional notes to Inta and to friends.

The writing of these pieces grew out of relationships with their teacher and fellow pupils. The three Blyton books read by the teacher provided the opportunity for significant group and sub-group literary experiences. What is of interest in the context of this book is that relationships of this type are

22. Blyton, *The Enchanted Wood*.

23. Seuss, *There's a Wocket in my Pocket*.

24. I have written in more detail about this case of Blyton intertextuality elsewhere. See, for example, Cairney, *Pathways to Literacy*.

25. Blyton, *The Enchanted Wood*.

at work in all classrooms. Some are visible to the teacher, some are not. Some are sanctioned, others are not. Some support the curriculum initiatives of the teacher, others do not.[26] What is critical to whether such relationships support or counteract the curriculum is the teacher's pedagogy, not their curriculum and methods. Some will perhaps guess that Inta was embracing an approach to curriculum that was fairly child-centered and that employed a writers' workshop approach to the curriculum. But this approach—let's call it an approach to curriculum or methodology—might well have been conducted in a very different way depending on the teacher's personal pedagogy.

Inta's classroom was shaped by a number of key pedagogical assumptions about learning and this had an impact on practices in relation to classroom management, use of space, the forms of interaction permitted, and rules for its conduct, access to resources, interaction patterns, and so on.

The popularity of the Blyton look-alikes was a natural outgrowth of a pedagogy that allowed a specific group interest to be shared by members of the class. It was a pedagogy informed by educational theory and views on learning, but also Inta's Christian faith, and her recognition that every child in her care was unique, precious in the sight of God, and capable of original and creative thought. This vignette demonstrates how curriculum content, methodological knowledge, and educational purpose informed by faith come together to create unique contexts and rich outcomes. I will return to Inta's classroom later in the chapter to elaborate further.

The challenge for Christian schools is to create authentic communities that are situated in-between two worlds. One of the dangers is that what we do will focus on this world, rather than the world to come. The school is expected to prepare children for the life of this world, but for the Christian school this should always be understood as a life that is in preparation for the coming kingdom of God. Our schools must be places that are shaped with an understanding of the words of John the Baptist, that we are to be people who, in humility, "repent, for the kingdom of heaven is at hand" (Matt 3:2). Our task is to create communities in which obstacles are removed that might hinder our students' reception of the kingdom of God.

---

26. I have written about the way in which at times classrooms can have an underground curriculum that operates separate from the mandated and official curriculum. See for example Cairney, "Supporting the Independent Learners," 78–96.

One of the greatest obstacles is a failure to grasp that they are meant for greater things than just fun in the sun.

There is a famous piece of graffiti on the seawall facing Australia's iconic Bondi Beach that trumpets to all who pass this idyllic spot, "Live like it's heaven on earth."[27] The sentiment of this slogan is that earth is heaven, so we should live life accordingly. But the reality is we are an in-between people, living on earth, which will one day face judgment, but with the certain hope that "everyone who calls on the name of the Lord will be saved" (Rom 10:13). The Christian's hope is one day we will live eternally in a new heaven and a new earth that awaits us when Jesus returns to judge the world.

Just as believers in Christ are to be in-between people, our Christian schools must also be in-between places or spaces. As the prophet Isaiah makes clear to the Jewish nations, a party awaits us in heaven, not on earth (Isa 24–25). Doug Blomberg, in his book *Wisdom and Curriculum*, suggests the task of the Christian school is to use curriculum (which he defines as "the relationship between the teacher and the child"[28]) to create

> a (school-)world within the world, because it is a selection from and sequencing of an all-but-infinite range of possible experiences. It is a conscious (re-)ordering of the world for the purposes of teaching and learning. The ends to which these processes are directed provide the criteria for the selection and organization of school experience.[29]

A key argument in this book is Christian schooling must do more than just give knowledge of the world that will empower; it must present a different perspective of the world and humankind's purpose within it. The nurturing of faith in Christ is central to the Christian classroom and school. But this is not simply about teaching catechisms, Bible stories, biblical propositions, and doctrine. Biblical knowledge is of course a foundation of faith, but it needs to be embedded within Christian communities that reflect a school culture that is different from the world. As I have already suggested, such communities of learners shaped by Christian teachers will serve as their own apologetic, pointing students toward truths not yet known. There will be a pedagogy adopted by teachers and promoted by the

27. I'm grateful to a previous pastor of my church, Rev. John Smuts, for pointing this mural out.

28. Blomberg, *Wisdom and Curriculum*, 4

29. Ibid., 17.

school that will in varied ways reinforce, support, and teach a different view of humanity and God's purposes for us. But how? And what might this culture-building within Christian schools look like?

Nicholas Wolterstorff offers us some clues in his book *Educating for Shalom: Essays on Christian Higher Education*. His reflections on university education in the United States center on "public piety," which he recognizes has given ground to anti-religion and secularist views. He concludes that the life of the campus can be shaped by a "cluster of beliefs, goals, rituals, symbols, and objects of veneration."[30] Institutions should educate for *shalom*. For as he suggests, to "dwell in *shalom* is to find delight in living rightly in one's physical surroundings, to find delight in living rightly with one's fellow human beings, to find delight even in living rightly with oneself."[31]

Wolterstorff's ideas are just as relevant for schools. Some might suggest his ideas are similar to virtues, values, and worldview-based approaches. However, he offers insights which I believe go deeper in shaping the culture of any institution. In effect, what he suggests is really a type of active social ethic, and patterns of reasoning that can have the effect of encouraging attentiveness to the world. This in turn can lead to the observation and embracing of the commendable life of the community, consistent with the institutional goals for life in the world and their hoped-for future.[32]

Stanley Hauerwas says something not too dissimilar to Wolterstorff in his book *The State of the University: Academic Knowledges and the Knowledge of God*. He suggests teachers in secondary schools often repeat the mistakes and miseducation they learned at universities, and that "any knowledge worth having cannot help but shape who we are and accordingly our understanding of the world." This, he suggests, is a type of "moral formation rather than education."[33]

James K. A. Smith, in an address at New College in 2012, helpfully outlined how the Christian school is a type of hybrid institution that sits within two ecosystems. It is an educational institution linked to many others of like type. Hence, some of its identity and makeup reflects what is common to all such institutions and which are influenced by various forces. But he suggests there is another ecosystem.[34]

30. Wolterstorff, *Educating for Shalom*, 5.

31. Ibid., 23.

32. Ibid., 144–50.

33. Hauerwas, *The State of the University*, 46.

34. James Smith, "Sanctified Perception," n.p.

On the other hand, a Christian school is a *Christian* school, which situates us in the ecosystem of the church and various other institutions of Christian mission. So, the Christian school is located at the intersection of these two ecosystems, and it is precisely this hybridity that generates the unique mission and task of Christian education.[35]

James Smith's ideas are well articulated in his book *Desiring the Kingdom*,[36] where he argues that the task of Christian education is not just the training and filling of minds with knowledge. Rather, it is about formation and the shaping of desire. Education is to be formative, providing knowledge, but also shaping one's orientation to the world.

Smith points out what should be obvious to us: the competitor for Christian education is not secular education, but rather competing pedagogies of desire that operate within the world and across cultures. He suggests the multiple contexts provide secular liturgies in which we are immersed. And these he suggests, "covertly form our loves."[37] Our students inhabit many spaces and communities of practice. Whether with friends hanging out in the mall, in the pinball parlor as was my experience as a child, online with Facebook friends, or in any number of settings where people interact, our interests and desires are formed. We participate in numerous and varied communities of practice where we share with others and are being formed with a desire for some version of the imagined good life.

In summation, while all of these writers have varied contexts into which they speak, all share an emphasis on connecting educational pedagogy with student lives with the hope of Christian formation. This chapter completes our detailed consideration of the definition of pedagogy that has shaped this book. We have considered how the *telos* of Christian education is centered on the kingdom of God, not just earthly success and achievement. We have considered the relationship between our priorities shaped by the gospel, our faith in Christ, how we live out and speak of this faith, and our actions. We have also considered how the things we teach and the way we do it cannot be separated from the life of the school community and the varied communities of practice our children inhabit. Chapter 4 will continue our consideration of pedagogy with special consideration of the role of the teacher and teaching.

35. Ibid., n.p.

36. Smith, *Desiring the Kingdom*.

37. Ibid., 24–27.

4

Pedagogy, Teaching, and the Kingdom

A doxological refrain pervades Augustine's Confessions; every good he experiences and all truth he learns come ultimately from God and are occasions for praise. God is the being "by whom all things are true that are true, and all things are good that are good."

—ARTHUR E. HOLMES[1]

In this chapter I pick up the challenge of chapter 3 for teachers and parents to see learning as embodied and situated within communities of learners living and learning together. At the center of all of this discussion will be the need for Christian schools to demonstrate that they are kingdom-focused. Building on the discussion of embodiment and enactment in chapters 1 and 2, and our discussion of standpoint and *telos* in chapter 3, I will explore the relationship between pedagogy and the community life of the classroom, and school and the role of the teacher. My argument introduced in the last chapter is the education of children should be informed by a coherent, implied (and sometimes explicit) understanding of the purpose and goal of their schooling. The intended goal of education, and the hoped-for future that is implied in all we do at school, has an important relationship to the type of community we create and of course our pedagogy. This chapter is also foundational to chapter 5 that will focus very much on the learner and learning.[2]

1. Holmes, *Building the Christian Academy*, 26.

2. I owe a great debt of gratitude to James Smith, whose book *Desiring the Kingdom:*

EDUCATING THE WHOLE CHILD

God Made Us as Holistic Creatures

At the New College Lectures in 2012, James K. A. Smith argued education is a "holistic endeavor" with a focus on formation of the child.[3] Teachers and our students all vary in our characteristics, abilities, and features, but the sum of all we are is seen in our unique identities. The elements of our wholeness include the body, mind, desires, and imagination. As such, our efforts to educate children should reflect more of this holism. However, as Smith rightly points out, under the influence of Platonism for more than two thousand years, there has been a common separation of mind and body, whether implied or explicit. Associated with this, he argues, there has been a separation of the categories of thought and action, belief and reason, word and deed. The consequence of such separation has been the development of rationalist views of the world and the education of children as if they are little more than "cognitive machines."[4] Such a limited view of humanity, if uncontested, has many consequences for educational practice.

One of the most obvious consequences of such a separation of mind and body is education can quickly become synonymous with intellectual content, academic achievement, and a consequential shift of educational emphasis to method and curriculum. This always heralds an inevitable drift by teachers towards the preferential consideration of what and how they teach, with less concern for why.

But not only this, some faith-based educational institutions begin to assume specific methods are more biblical than others. For example, some have suggested if our quest is one of formation rather than personal discovery, should we adopt teacher-centered approaches and shun child-focused approaches to learning? As well, does the focus on formation lead to a caution with creative approaches to curriculum, child-centered learning, and pedagogy that allows too much self-choice and self-direction? My short answer is no! There should be encouragement of children to use their

---

Worship, Worldview, and Cultural Formation, had a significant impact on how I have been able to reconcile my biblical understanding of our humanity and God's purpose for his people with secular work research on pedagogy, learning, and teaching. I had the privilege of hosting him at my university in 2012 to run a series of public lectures. The chance to meet with him and ask many questions about each other's work was invaluable.

3. James Smith, "Erotic Comprehension," 6.

4. James Smith, *Desiring the Kingdom,* 41–43.

God-given imaginations, we should create environments in which discovery learning is possible and where students can pursue learning that motivates them. We are made in God's image and our creativity, inquisitiveness, problem-solving abilities, and self-motivation are gifts God has given us that reflect something of his character.

Emphatic and dogmatic conclusions about teaching methods ignore the complexity and diversity of human abilities and nature, as well as how humans learn and what the Bible teaches about our humanity. God offers us freedom, rather than simply restriction in what and how we teach, and this includes the way teachers support and shape learning and formation. We can observe varying approaches to teaching and learning in the Bible, but it does not prescribe optimal methods and does not promote separation of body and mind. In fact, from beginning to end it has much to say about the complexity of the people God made, their embodiment, and the varied ways he works in their lives. I will of course return to these discussions later.

To understand what Christian pedagogy looks like, which in turn shapes our teaching, we need first to consider our personhood, specifically the people God made us to be. For as James Smith reminds us, we are not simply "thinking machines."[5] We are "believing creatures" with creative capacities, imaginations, and the ability to love, hate, laugh, and cry. So, in considering pedagogy oriented to the kingdom of God, a biblical understanding of our humanity and personhood is vital. In the simplest of terms, what our teaching and pedagogy looks like requires us to understand who we teach.

How does a Biblical Anthropology Help Inform Us?

The quote at the beginning of this chapter from Arthur Holmes reminds us all truth comes from God. This is a key part of our humanity, a humility before our Creator, for all that is good and all that is true comes from him. I am indebted to Dr. Michael Jensen for his insights concerning our personhood. He challenged me to consider a theological anthropology of personhood as a key to my exploration of pedagogy.[6] As part of my work with the Anglican Education Fellowship (AEF)[7] mentioned earlier in this

---

5. Ibid., 43.

6. Cairney et al., *New Perspectives in Anglican Education.*

7. I describe the work and outcomes of the AEF in more detail in chapter 1.

book, Dr. Jensen reminded us of some key biblical truths that should shape the way we see our personhood and that of our students.

First among these is that true knowledge of ourselves is not possible without first knowing God, an insight we owe to John Calvin in the sixteenth century.[8] This of course was reprised by Oliver O'Donovan in his seminal work *Resurrection and Moral Order*, where he pointed to the foundational place of the resurrection in Christian ethics. Understanding our anthropology hinges very much on the resurrection of Jesus from the dead.[9] If we don't know God, the truth about who we are and who we can become is masked. But the Spirit of God can shine a light on our true character. To know who we are helps us know who we can become, and the same applies to our students. As we understand more about who we are, and what God wants for his creatures, we begin to have greater insight into the type of community life we create in schools and its purpose. I want to outline just five fundamental biblical insights that are important when considering our personhood and in helping to frame our pedagogy. First, a simple list, and then a short explanation of each:

1. We are God's creation, made and known by him.

2. God desires that we seek knowledge and wisdom from him.

3. The knowledge and learning that God's creatures seek is good.

4. God made us for relationship and as learners and doers.

5. Humans are imperfect and our lives are affected by sin.

First, foundational to our humanity is that we are God's creation, made by him and known by him. As James Smith reminds us, we are creatures with desires.[10] But we are sinful creatures, and without God's intervention our rebellion seeks to relegate his purposes beneath our own. But ultimately our future is still in God's hands; we do not control our own destinies. Indeed, Moses called on God and asked him to teach his people to number their days that they might gain hearts of wisdom (Ps 90). This is a lesson we are slow to learn, even though we were made "in the image and likeness of God" as spiritual beings to rule over creation. But this of course was for God's own purpose and good pleasure, not our own (Gen 1:26–28).

---

8. Calvin, *Institutes of the Christian Religion*, 37.

9. O'Donovan, *Resurrection and Moral Order*, 422.

10. James Smith, *Desiring the Kingdom*, 37–63.

Second, God also made us as creatures who are meant to know things. God's word teaches us much about knowledge, including its source and purpose. Ultimately, as Augustine taught us and as the Scriptures testify, all knowledge, wisdom, and truth comes from God, who is the author of all truth. And God has equipped mankind with the capacity to know and reason so we might be able to create, remember, solve problems, imagine, and discover. Of course this is not a quest to be as clever or to know as much as God, for this is impossible. Ecclesiastes reminds us God has "set eternity in the hearts of men; yet they cannot fathom what God has done from the beginning to the end" (Eccl 3:11).

Third, God sees all he made as good, and wants us to learn and explore our world. He sees the learning and knowledge of his creatures as good, and it is useful in the world. But of course, we know from various verses in Proverbs that God gives us knowledge as a gift, and not just for our own sake. There is always a relationship between the knowledge and wisdom that God gives and our relationship to him. Knowledge should draw us to God, not away from him. Proverbs 2:6 tells us, "For the Lord gives wisdom; from his mouth come knowledge and understanding." God also gives knowledge and wisdom to us for life purposes. As we live in his world in ways that honor him, we are to use our knowledge for good and his glory. In fact, we are to excel in this as in other qualities given to us as an act of grace. When Paul wrote to the Corinthian church (2 Cor 8:7), he listed knowledge as one of the human qualities they should have and excel in:

> But as you excel in everything—in faith, in speech, in knowledge,
> in all earnestness, and in our love for you—see that you excel in
> this act of grace also.

So too, schools should see knowledge as a gift from God, but our ultimate purpose is to see such knowledge used for God's good purposes, not self-glory or the honor simply of the school. There is a fine line between honoring God with the knowledge he gives us and self-glorification, as Psalm 10:4 warns:

> In his pride the wicked man does not seek him; in all his thoughts
> there is no room for God.

Fourth, God made us as social beings to be in relationship with him and each other. There is a personal and relational dimension to life and education that runs counter to pedagogy centered on the individual. Education is a gift from God to us, not just for our own benefit, but also for the good of others. We are communal creatures meant to be with others and building relationships with one another. Language and communication are also gifts that allow us to know, work with, and commune with one another. From the very beginning God saw "it is not good that man should be alone" (Gen 2:18). While humans can learn alone, teaching usually takes place in relationship to other people, first within the family, and later with other teachers and fellow learners.

Fifth, because of sin, evil and death are part of life and we will all face judgment, for the world is already under the sentence of this judgment. As a consequence, work is hard and life can have many frustrations. Sin also corrupted families as we read in the account of Cain and Abel in Genesis 4. When Cain and Abel brought offerings to the Lord, "The Lord looked with favor on Abel and his offering, but on Cain and his offering he did not look with favor. So Cain was very angry, and his face was downcast." (Gen 4:4b–5) Then the Lord said to Cain "Why are you angry? Why is your face downcast? If you do what is right, will you not be accepted? But if you do not do what is right, sin is crouching at your door; it desires to have you, but you must rule over it." (Gen 4:6b–7) But Cain lured Abel into the field and killed him (Gen 4:8).

But while the entry of sin into the world led to less-than-perfect families and communities, Michael Jensen reminds us they are still a means God uses to ameliorate the effects of sin in our lives and to bring blessing.[11] And just as communities outside the school are less than perfect, so too those within schools are imperfect. But through them, God may be revealed and our students nurtured in the imitation of Christ. Our hope is that within our schools our children will have an openness to seek salvation in Christ and become 'new creations' in him. For as Paul reminded the church in Corinth, " Therefore, if anyone is in Christ, the new creation has come: The old has gone, the new is here!" (2 Cor 5:17). Our desire and hope as Christian teachers should be that our students will seek to imitate Jesus in service, self-sacrifice, generosity and the forgiveness of others. This is the basis of community in the Christian school.

Finally, just as human sin was to distort the very communities which God created for us, it was also to distort the desires that drive our ambitions, hopes, and behavior. James Smith[12] reminds us that while the Bible teaches the object of our desires should first be God, we seek other things.

11. Cairney et al., *New Perspectives in Anglican Education*, 54.
12. James Smith, *Desiring the Kingdom*, 46–52.

The Bible has many references to what the focus of our desire should be. Perhaps the best known is Psalm 37:4: "Take delight in the Lord, and he will give you the desires of your heart." But while this verse is well known, it is often misunderstood. Many see it as suggesting that if you love and take delight in God, he will give you the desires of your heart. Hence dedication and obedience lead to reward. But this is an upside-down interpretation of what the psalmist means. The reality is the verse is suggesting if you place your delight in God, and he is the desire of your heart, then he will reshape what we see as important. We don't simply delight in who God is so he can grant us our desires! For as Jesus warned the Pharisees and teachers, the human heart cannot be trusted:

> For out of the heart come evil thoughts—murder, adultery, sexual immorality, theft, false testimony, slander. (Matt 15:19)

No, if we delight in God and have a relationship with him, in and through Christ, he will reshape our distorted desires to desire what he desires for us. James Smith suggests education needs to have an implied understanding of humanity that is more reflective of Augustine's argument that man's primary orientation to the world is not knowledge or belief, but rather love. It was Augustine who suggested "I am what I love."[13] Whether these practices are within the school, home, or community, they have an impact on our hoped-for goals (*telos*) and desires. Within our schools, we need to ask what are the desires that give shape to communities of practice in this classroom and school, how are these translated into the very goals of our institutions, and how does this influence the things our students value and desire?

Let me again stress that a biblical understanding of personhood should challenge us to rethink pedagogy. How we understand the children we teach will have a big impact on the type of classrooms and schools we create and the priorities that give direction to them.[14] What is the type of life that characterizes our schools, and what impact is this having on the formation of these young people and their hoped-for futures? An important question for all schools and teachers then is what is the ultimate vision of the good life we offer? What is it we project in the moment-to-moment activities of each day, and what motivates us as we seek to craft these communities to

13. Ibid., 46.

14. Cairney et al., *New Perspectives in Anglican Education*.

shape our students' desires and hoped-for futures? And finally, how is this reflected in our pedagogy?[15]

UNDERSTANDING HOW PEDAGOGY INTERSECTS WITH DIFFERENT WORLDS

It is important to recognize that the motivations of parents, students, and teachers do not always align. While this might be seen simply as a reality that we cannot avoid, good pedagogy requires an understanding of the disparate and at times conflicting desires and motivations of parents, students, and teachers. Perhaps more than at any time in human history, education is very much focused on knowledge and learning to serve success in the world. Rarely is learning seen as good in and of itself. Education has become more utilitarian as our students learn to seek personal success above all else. However, as we discussed in chapter 3, our task is not simply the intellectual growth of young minds. The foundations of modern faith-based schooling should echo the Greek concept of *paidagogeo*. This was a word rich in meaning and suggested an education that required the leading of the child in a process of growth in body, mind, and spirit.

Children were not assumed simply to make their own way, but were led into a community of scholars. So too, the key pedagogical idea that sits at the center of the type of school communities I am proposing seeks full student participation in the life of community. While much of what we do in schools may seem individualistic and related to just a fragment of our students' lives, hopes, and desires, the Christian school is to seek higher purposes and more ambitious outcomes. A key part of the task of the Christian school must surely be to help our students not just to survive at school, but to be equipped and supported as they inhabit and negotiate the multiple worlds that are part of their lives. Their growth in character is just as important as their growth in knowledge.

Paul reminded the church in Rome that when faced with the at times unhelpful distractions of the world, our very bodies—our complete selves—are in effect meant to be our "living sacrifices, holy and pleasing to God" (Rom 12:1). There is a connection between mind, word, and action. Schools are to be concerned with the whole person.

The Christian school also has an important responsibility to support parents in the challenging task of raising their children. We will do this as

15. James Smith, *Desiring the Kingdom*, 40–43.

teachers who hopefully understand that our very lives, not just our words and our will, help our children grow in their understanding of God's kingdom. Our role as teachers is to create classrooms and school communities that help students seek the kingdom of God, and to see the good it promises as something to be desired above all things. Such a school community commends children to consider a different life driven by different desires and purposes.

David Hohne draws upon 1 Peter 2 to offer an insight into the type of life Scripture commends to all of his followers, and how lives lived in community impact others. The Christian life is one shaped by careful consideration of attitudes and behavior. Our lives, and the lives of our communities, should demonstrate "a beautiful way of life" echoing the words of Peter to the churches in Asia.[16] Our students, not just teachers, can speak into the lives of others. The Apostle Peter commended in his letter that followers of Christ should

> Live such good lives among the pagans that, though they accuse
> you of doing wrong, they may see your good deeds and glorify
> God on the day he visits us. (1 Pet 2:12 ESV)

Hohne argues that we need a "theological description of human learning, knowing and understanding."[17] By this he is arguing along with Colin Gunton,[18] James Smith,[19] and many others for a proper understanding of the relationship between reason, perception, and the indwelling of the world. Michael Polanyi's work has relevance to this discussion as well, particularly his writing on rehabituation of belief as critical to knowledge and action. Polanyi reminded us that our "tacit powers" dictate our adherence to cultural practices by sustaining our intellectual, artistic, civic, and religious existence within them.[20]

Within our schools, learning can result from the transforming experience of both body and mind, and lead to new habits that are in relationship with one another. Knowledge of significance of practices within communities is acquired within the context of relationships of significance, and has meaning for members of these shared groups. And of course, as we have

---

16. Hohne, "Becoming an Apologetic Person," 4–9.

17. Ibid., 4

18. Gunton, "Knowledge and Culture," 99.

19. James Smith, *Desiring the Kingdom*, 75–88.

20. Polanyi, *Personal Knowledge*, 264.

already discussed, our children have membership in multiple communities, many invisible to the teacher and the school. Such a view of education should offer little credence to slavish adherence to one right method, or a single best approach to learning; more nuanced interpretations are needed.

As discussed in chapter 2, all humans are embedded within multiple communities and each community has its own sets of social practices. Jean Lave and Etienne Wenger use the term "communities of practice" to refer to groups that share a concern or a passion for something they do, learning how to do it better as they interact regularly.[21] Understanding how groups begin to assume particular ways of doing things, we inevitably come back to shared hopes, goals, loves, and desires which ultimately lead to common daily practices that become normative.

While Lave and Wenger speak of shared passion or concern, as I mentioned above, James Smith focuses on human desire as a key source of life direction and purpose. He warns us that if we fail to understand humans are creatures of desire, we may end up instead seeing them simply as cognitive beings driven by "thought and rational operations."[22] This type of thinking will ultimately lead to forms of education that become detached from the communities which children see as significant, have commitment to, and learn from. The resulting effect is the education offered has little impact on their formation.

In its most extreme form, education that fails to view learners as creatures with hopes and desires, who seek communion with others, and who share community practices of significance, will fail to have an impact on lives beyond securing assent to practices to which there is little commitment. Education of this type leaves little space for the questions, doubts or dissent to be expressed, and minimal intersection with young lives. If this is the nature of education, children's questions and the desires of their heart are not addressed, or worse still, their questions are left unasked and hence unanswered. Education like this fails to grasp that God shows his grace and kindness to us by teaching us not as isolated individual minds, but as embodied creatures within the boundaries of families and schools which themselves are situated within the church of God. As James Smith argues, we are creatures "who make our way in the world more by feeling

---

21. Lave and Wenger, *Situated Learning*, 3–11.
22. James Smith, *Desiring the Kingdom*, 42.

our way around it . . . groping with our bodies," not simply thinking our way rationally around it.[23]

The role of the Christian teacher is to endeavor to orchestrate a lived experience for their students that will present God to them in a biblically consistent manner. This will always be embedded within a complex web of relationships and competing views of the world. This is a big task, which is why throughout this book I am at pains to stress that why we teach is more critical to children's spiritual growth and formation of their characters than what and how we teach. The more foundational why and what for questions often remain unanswered or perhaps not even asked.[24]

The pedagogy I am advocating in this book is not an intellectual concept to be debated and then ignored; it is one that should transform how teachers see their role. In turn, it will hopefully challenge them to create a specific type of learning community within their classroom that is connected to the numerous other communities of practice of which their students are part. This is an enacted pedagogy that requires the integration of knowing, being, and acting.

In a sense, Christian pedagogy requires the teacher to maintain a metaphorical community orchestra made of the key instruments of teaching, learning, knowledge, intent, and over all of these, belief. It is her or his role to conduct this integrated metacommunity for the good. The Christian pedagogue is seeking in all they do within the classroom to challenge the very foundations of desire, and appeal to a humanity that is as rich as the Bible's teaching on personhood and God's purposes for creating and sustaining us. Douglas Barnes, whose work was discussed in chapters 2 and 3, wouldn't have agreed with the emphasis on God and didn't specifically use the word *pedagogy*, but he understood the communicative life of the classroom had a powerful impact on students. Combined with what we know of human desire and God's purposes, we are armed with an important foundation for grasping just how important pedagogy is and how potentially narrow and limiting the term "curriculum" can be, a point to which I will return later.

23. Ibid., 47.

24. Asking better questions is an important part of pedagogy. For a more detailed discussion of the art of questioning, visit my blog that supports this book at http://pedagogyandformation.blogspot.com.au/.

PEDAGOGY AND THE TEACHER

To be a Christian school is to be a different school, not just in the results we achieve academically, or socially in the leadership roles our graduates take on, but in how the very institution is used redemptively by God. This is not just seen in the lives of the students and families associated with the school, but in the wider community and indeed through the lives of graduating students throughout the world. In chapter 9, we will discuss, how schools equip students for such a life.

When looked at from the perspective of the teacher, we could conclude that reconciling faith and practice is all too difficult. Hence, some teachers simply retreat to being a Christian who teaches well (with varied meaning). Some Christian schools don't even prioritize faith when choosing teachers, though most would look for an acceptance of the *ethos* and goals of the school. But as I have argued already, if you are a Christian teacher, then you are called to be a different type of teacher. A Christian teacher should be someone who is being transformed into the likeness of Christ, one who is different in character, motivations, moral views, and purposes. As well, the Christian teacher will want to see students transformed in more than just their knowledge and skills. The formation of the child will be their priority, and of course an understanding of the nature of learning should inform their pedagogy.

The Christian teacher should be one who, in teaching children, reaches qualitatively different decisions day by day as he or she nurtures and teaches the children God has entrusted to them. This is not meant to imply our decisions will always be different from those of the non-Christian teacher, for they too can make right decisions based on their knowledge of curriculum, teaching, learning, and pedagogy. Once again, this is a case of common grace in action, for they also were made in the image of God. But the Christian teacher should start with an awareness that just as the Bible offers us guidance on how not to act, it also teaches us how "*to act*" as a child of God (Eph 4:17–5:21). I believe the Bible offers wisdom that enables teachers to make wise choices day by day as they make decisions about what and how they teach. And of course, what gives ultimate shape to their pedagogy will be the reasons they make the choices they do. What is the ultimate purpose of their teaching, what is the hoped-for future they see for their students? Does this role require all teachers to be Christians in a Christian school? Ideally yes, for while the non-Christian teacher may well be equally committed to formation, they will inevitably be focused on different end goals. This of course will be a decision for every Christian school to make.

The Christian teacher needs to have the desired character, faith, and abilities to lead their children toward an awareness of, and focus on, the kingdom of God. As well, they must have the required knowledge of curriculum and learning, and the ability to teach! Just as Christian schools are to be different and distinctive, Christian teachers are also to be different. Robert Pazmino suggests this distinctiveness should flow from our understanding of the Scriptures.[25] But what does this mean? I have seen teachers with good biblical understanding, strong faith, and a godly life who have not taught well or even authentically. Is the key that the Christian teacher should hold a particular set of values and character traits that shape their character and how they teach? Well, yes and no. Our values will influence character, and should influence how we structure curriculum and make choices in the classroom, but our faith must be more than just a filter for accepting or discarding the confusing mix of options thrown up by educational research.

Is worldview the key? There are schools that place great emphasis on staff holding a particular worldview as a foundation of its authentic education. But a visit to many Christian school websites quickly show that if there has been an attempt to stress a biblical foundation for what the school does, this can be shallow and limiting. Worse still, some school aims will often be stated in theological language that was never meant to shape action, or at best would be hard to translate into action. Too many schools and teachers fail to move from the generalities of school aims, syllabus requirements, trusted methods, and personal beliefs to a concern for how curriculum is enacted each day and the pedagogical practices that shape the culture of classrooms and schools.

As I said at the beginning of this chapter, above all else, the Christian teacher's role is to create a classroom environment (a community of practice) in which children grow in body, mind, and soul. At the core of this is the extent to which all the teacher does communicates the wisdom of God revealed in Christ.

Using the Bible almost as a textbook to shape teaching and learning is not what is required. In effect, if we do this, we commit two fundamental errors. First, as I have already argued in earlier chapters, while the why and what for of our pedagogy will be shaped by our biblical knowledge, there

25. Pazmino, *Foundational Issues in Christian Education*, 57–83.

is little justification in trying to do the same to what we teach and how we teach it. Notwithstanding the truth that in the life of the classroom, every action of the teacher can in a sense point to the good, shaping curriculum artificially is unwise.

The danger is that in seeking to shape curriculum and teaching methods within a biblical framework to control content and method, we might simply make a different type of rationalistic error in seeking to teach the right ideas in the right way. In doing this, my contention is the school will have no better chance of capturing the hearts and minds of our students. In effect, we will end up simply replacing one set of ideas with another. A different set of propositions or presuppositions—perhaps labeled as worldview, values, ethics, or even virtues—will replace one curriculum with another, with no greater chance of student transformation.

James Smith reminds us that worldview talk has "misconstrued the nature and task of Christian education because the operative notion of worldview at work there has been tied to a stunted, rationalistic picture of the human person."[26] Our aim as Christian educators must be much more than to transmit knowledge and information in the hope of transformation. Instead, we must keep coming back to why we teach, not simply what and how we teach, and to the *telos* that drives us and our students.

A second error with the shaping of content and method within a narrow biblical framework is it operates within rather disembodied and individualistic assumptions of personhood, with reduced or little attention or connection between thought and action. Hence, education becomes a question of how we connect faith with the broad curriculum or the nature of institutions like the church and school.[27] This is similar to the error of most presuppositionalist arguments. Presuppositionalists in their most extreme form believe we need to employ distinctively Christian principles in order to genuinely know. That is, they believe specific assumptions, standards, and knowledge influence one's epistemic activity. Our beliefs are assumed to lead to a distinctively Christian way of doing everything. John Frame concludes, for example, in *Five Views on Apologetics*, that all claims to knowledge "are governed by presuppositions" and that as a result it is difficult for any person to be simply "neutral."[28] While I acknowledge that Christians and non-Christians do differ in whom and what we give

---

26. James Smith, *Desiring the Kingdom*, 32.

27. Ibid., pp 44–46.

28. Frame, "Presuppositional Apologetics," 226–27.

allegiance to, I don't accept that there is no neutral ground or common knowledge between us. As Dani Scarratt suggests, "Much of what is known by Christians will be genuinely known by non-Christians for the same reasons and in the same way."[29]

Summing up, I am arguing that the role of the teacher is not to apply a biblical filter to judge the rightness of every activity, method, or classroom practice.[30] Rather, the Christian teacher is called to be a different type of teacher, one who is first being transformed into the likeness of Christ, with character and motivations that reflect their faith. Such a teacher will want to see students transformed in more than just their knowledge and skills, but dogmatic conclusions about which teaching method should be used is simply a blind alley. There is freedom in method, curriculum content, and classroom practices.[31] The Christian teacher will as a professional be concerned with what and how they teach, but of foundational importance is why they do so. It is the latter that should drive their actions as a teacher.

As I have already stated above, the role of the Christian teacher is to do their best to orchestrate the classroom and school in order to point their students toward Christ. This will always be embedded within a complex web of relationships and competing views of the world. But there is no doubt the Christian teacher will make qualitatively different decisions each day as she nurtures and teaches the children God has entrusted to her.

29. Scarratt, "Unearthing the Presuppositions of Presuppositionalism," 13.

30. The above arguments of course do not mention the mandates of curriculum that may also influence the what and how of teaching.

31. Again, I should comment that there is less freedom in relation to content with secondary students or where school systems have mandated curriculum content.

5

Meaning, Learning, and Formation

Beneath the level of norms, roles, institutional structures, rituals, stories, and symbols lies the level of our fundamental communal intentions toward one another and the world, which govern how we live in our roles and rituals and by means of which we apprehend the mystery of our existence.[1]

—CRAIG DYKSTRA

As discussed briefly in chapter 4, schools communites have added complexity due to students' concurrent membership of many diverse communities, a veritable patchwork of overlapping groups. Life is shared in meaningful ways as students exchange ideas, loves, and desires inside and outside the precincts of the school. As Kevin Vanhoozer reminds us, our everyday world includes "the moral, intellectual, and spiritual atmosphere in which we live."[2] But while we share a similar context with others, "we inhabit it differently."[3] As we share common practices, concerns, and desires with others, we might also enter into their cultural worlds as well and begin to take on shared ideas. Our students make, share, and communicate meaning with others and are in part formed by these transactions as they interact and exchange values and views of the world. Meaning itself is actually being tested in such exchanges, shared and even negotiated with others! What is right or wrong, appropriate or inappropriate, false or true, are subject to

---

1. Dykstra, *Growing in the Life of Faith*, xi.
2. Vanhoozer, "What is Everyday Theology?," 19.
3. Ibid., 19.

negotiation, consensus, or disagreement. The teacher, as an active observer within the classroom, needs to extend their observational interests to include the formation of our students in these rich social worlds. How our students reconcile and make sense of these competing views of the world, and how this is influenced by others, should be of considerable interest to teachers. While much of this is played out in the minds and private lives of our students, it is possible to observe tell-tale signs of shifts in the loves and desires of our students.

THE RELATIONSHIP OF FAITH TO THE SOCIAL CONSTRUCTION OF MEANING

Etienne Wenger suggests, "Human engagement in the world is first and foremost a process of negotiating meaning."[4] In life, there is sustained attention, readjustment, resistance, and malleability going on as this occurs. Members are affecting and being affected in a continuous interaction as the negotiation of multiple meanings takes place. However, in stressing the constructive and social nature of meaning, he concludes that

> from this perspective, meaning is always the product of its negotiation, by which I mean that it exists in a process of negotiation.[5]

Such a statement can be read as precluding or denying the status of the eternal truths that are the basis of faith and faith-based communities. However, Wenger suggests, a little confusingly, that meaning is "simply made up."[6] I want to challenge the idea that meaning is always a "continuous process of renewed negotiation."[7] While I believe seeking after knowledge and truth does involve negotiation, Wenger's comments cast doubt on how he views truth. At the very least, his description places doubt on whether he sees a place for truth. In a world that has just invented the phrase "alternative facts," this needs to be contested on behalf of teachers who have a faith basis to their lives. Is the life, death, and resurrection of Jesus, as suggested by the Scriptures and other evidence, truth, or simply a negotiated meaning? There is a big difference between Christians agreeing that on balance Jesus rose from the dead, and instead, believing it to be true. Having said

4. Wenger, *Communities of Practice*, 53.

5. Ibid., 54.

6. Ibid., 54.

7. Ibid., 54.

this, of course science and religion must always be open to testing previously understood truths. But am I suggesting our aim is to indoctrinate young minds with Christian truths? No!

The work of Elmer Thiessen on open-mindedness and indoctrination is helpful for grasping this point. Thiessen argues that to be open to the ideas of others is a good thing, and that "open-mindedness is closely related to critical thinking."[8] Drawing wisdom from Socrates's well-known statement that "the unexamined life is not worth living," he suggests that "open-mindedness means openness to critical reflection concerning one's own beliefs and those of others."[9] Thiessen reminds us that simply presenting Christian truth in an authoritative way "will of necessity discourage critical openness." In Thiessen's view, if critical openness is promoted in our schools, then claims of indoctrination have no grounds.[10] There is a very real sense in which every person needs to reach a point of deciding themselves whether Jesus is true or not. Ultimately, it will be the work of the Spirit that leads people to the truth, but we must hold to the understanding that there are truths, and there is a need to cultivate open-mindedness within our schools. The aim is for Christian truths to be discussed and considered, not simply silently dismissed or compliantly mouthed.

One of the great dangers in Christian schools is the temptation to wage a war against cultural practices that are seen as inconsistent with the faith. Faith is not just a set of practices that together enables us to label a group of people. If we think we can teach culture, we miss the fact that culture is not simply a noun, it can also be a verb! It is agreed by scholars that culture is "an integrated pattern of human knowledge, belief, and behavior,"[11] which of course can be learned and transmitted to succeeding generations. Of course, there are ways we would hope Christians would act. Following Kathryn Tanner's definition, that "culture can be understood as the meaning dimension of social life,"[12] Vanhoozer suggests "every part of life signifies something about the values and beliefs that shape culture. Therefore, every part of culture communicates something about the meaning of the

---

8. Thiessen, *Teaching for Commitment*, 148.

9. Ibid., 148.

10. Ibid., 168.

11. See Webster's online dictionary: https://www.merriam-webster.com/dictionary/culture.

12. Tanner, *Theories of Culture*, 31.

whole."[13] As teachers, we need to constantly read culture because as well as offering explicit messages, culture communicates basic orientations to life.

How the school manages and constructs the life of the school community and its interaction with and relationship to other diverse communities and sub-communities, as well as their culture and practices, is critical. As I have written elsewhere, "to be a teacher or a pupil in any school demands specific ways of using language, behaving, interacting, and adherence to sets of values and attitudes"[14] and beliefs. Linguist James Gee argued that schools engage in "particular" discourses. This concept of course has resonance with Etienne Wenger's concept of "communities of practice." Gee describes discourses as "ways of behaving, interacting, valuing, thinking, believing, speaking, and often reading and writing that are accepted as instantiations of particular roles (or "types" of people) by specific groups or people."[15]

Gee suggests that even the way we engage in school practices like reading and writing are the social constructs of specific groups. We could say the same for forms of public worship and many other cultural practices within our schools. Our students are enculturated into these practices and the meanings they embrace and communicate. Of course, this might simply involve a shared love of things that have no eternal significance like tastes in music, clothing, or food; however, these discourse communities might adopt habits and beliefs that extend to the exclusion of specific types of students, shared attitudes to learning, views on sexuality, dislike for a student or teacher, prejudices, and so on.

As a teacher within a Christian school we cannot accept negotiated views and responses to hatred, oppression, abuse, ridicule, exclusion, and so on.[16] We need to understand that many of the discourse communities in which our students share aspects of life are largely invisible to us. Martin Buber reminds us of the important role the teacher plays in the formation of the children in their care:

> What we term education, conscious and willed, means a selection by man [sic] of the effective world: it means to give decisive

13. Vanhoozer, "What is Everyday Theology?," 24.

14. Cairney, "Literacy Diversity," 44.

15. Gee, *Social Linguistics and Literacies*, viii–ix.

16. Of course, examples of these kinds are where understanding one's worldview and how it is based on the Scriptures is important.

effective power to a selection of the world which is concentrated and manifested in the educator.[17]

Such a view is of course at odds with some progressive attitudes to the role of the teacher, but the Christian school cannot avoid this responsibility.

Buber's comment highlights the importance of the role of the teacher and how we engage with our students as we shape school community practices. The challenge of course is that, as we have already discussed, classrooms are places where meanings are indeed being negotiated and agreed upon, and often while teachers and parents are completely unaware. Views of the world and all aspects of life are being reinforced as specific interactions between participants occur, and as teachers and students live out their daily lives. Snapchat conversations occur between members of friendship groups in an almost continuous stream of language, emojis,[18] and images.[19] Schools and classes may share many specific behaviors (like participant roles), organizational structures (such as grouping, teaching strategies) and resource characteristics (such as carefully chosen texts), but they are also characterized by unique communities of practice that reflect the way each student lives together with others of significance to them. Each will have particular group-shared understandings, ways of acting and responding, language, common goals, and desires that give shape to their lives outside, as well as inside, the classroom.

Negotiation is clearly an important part of school and classroom life. David Fernie, Bronwyn Davies, Paula McMurray, and Rebecca Kantor suggest that classroom life involves students negotiating roles, rights, obligations, norms, and expectations from different standpoints.[20] The teacher and students contribute to the context in which they learn, while they also negotiate roles and relationships and what counts as knowledge, culture, and belief. The application of a Christian pedagogy will hopefully show evidence of different responses, actions, and communications that seek to change behavior and attitudes to the world, as well as their character.

---

17. Buber, *Between Man and Man*, 106.

18. An emoji is a small digital image or icon used to express an idea or emotion in electronic communication.

19. This is reason enough to insist students either leave mobile phones at home or only use them in set lunch periods and when in transit to and from school. While there are challenges with this, it may be worth the effort and short-term pain.

20. Fernie et al., "Becoming a Person in the Preschool," 95–110.

Classroom life will evidence varied attitudes and worldviews, as students and the teacher negotiate how to live together.

ORCHESTRATING THE MEANING, LANGUAGE, AND LIFE OF THE CLASSROOM

A fundamental question for the faith-based school is how aware are parents and teachers of this rich daily negotiation of meaning between class members and their varied communities of practice? Furthermore, how much impact do the teaching, curriculum, and pedagogy of the teacher impact this shared view of the world that is developing? While Christian schools might have compulsory chapel, Bible study, and perhaps even home groups, do these groups achieve much more than an understanding or knowledge of beliefs, rules, and cultural practices with which they must comply while in the classroom or school? How aware are we as teachers and principals of the rest of our students' lives and the hold that emerging shared meanings, goals, loves, and life priorities might be having on their hearts, minds, and futures?

By paraphrasing the work of Edward Farley[21] in the quote that heads this chapter, Craig Dykstra offers some wise advice in relation to these matters. "Beneath the level of norms, roles, institutional structures, rituals, stories, and symbols lies the level of our fundamental communal intentions toward one another and the world, which govern how we live in our roles and rituals and by means of which we apprehend the mystery of our existence."[22] The following vignette might illustrate what this means in practice.

Vignette 5: Secret Codes and "Silent" Messages

In my first decade of teaching within schools, I had the privilege of being given charge of what we call in Australia a one-teacher school. This was a secular government school. Usually one-teacher schools are in remote or rural places and have a single classroom with children who can potentially be five to twelve years old. I arrived to find seventeen students across six grades in my first year. By my third year in the school, I had thirty-one

21. Farley, *Ecclesial Man*.
22. Dykstra, *Growing in the Life of Faith*, xi.

students across all seven elementary grades. I also had responsibility for the grounds, buildings, activities with the families, a parents' and citizens' group that met in the school, and so on. I had five kindergarten children and between two and five students in every other grade. As a result, I used a flexible ability group approach, with up to five groups for some subjects (such as mathematics, literacy, sports, and even library!). I also used independent learning assignments, mixed-ability groups for some work (e.g., social science, art, and music), and the occasional whole group lesson for things like poetry, craft, art, and literature appreciation.

A popular activity was literature when I read something to the whole school! I varied the books to cater as much as possible for the wide age range and interests. A favorite was the delightful picture book *Lester and Clyde*, written and illustrated by James Reece.[23] The book tells the story of two frogs who lived in a tranquil and idyllic pond. Lester was a young, energetic trickster, and Clyde, his friend, was older and more serious. Lester loved playing tricks on him. One day when Lester had played one too many practical jokes, his friend Clyde expelled him from the pond with the words, "You're a pest, you're a menace, you cannot live here." Clyde lived to regret this moment of frustration, because he missed Lester, even his impish behavior and tricks. Eventually they were reunited after Lester spent a day or two wandering in less idyllic parts where human intervention was destroying the wetlands. I had read the book on two or three occasions over two years, and some of the children had subsequently read the story for themselves.

One day, during a lesson of one sort or another that involved only part of the school, I noticed in my peripheral vision one of my third-graders (Phillip) was off-task, being his often impish and sometimes disruptive self. Quite spontaneously, I turned to him and began to quote some words from the story of *Lester and Clyde*. In my normal, but slightly-stern-for-a-teacher voice (for effect), I began to say loudly enough for all to hear, "Phillip, you're a pest, you're a menace . . ." But before I could finish the sentence, half the class chimed in with "you cannot live here!" This was the moment at which this quote was given new shared status as part of the community life and practice and it had become a secret code only we shared. Our understanding of this lovely story became enriched by this small, public, and shared enactment of our understanding and appreciation of the story, as well as each other as a community. Phillip, like Lester was prone to pranks and

23. Reece, *Lester and Clyde*.

acts of mischief and distraction, and he could even be a touch annoying, but we still loved him and saw him as part of our community in this small rural school. As well, our understanding of the story was enriched by the conflation of a real-life mischief-maker and a literary mischief-maker. And this secret code was now one of the many markers that set us apart as co-members of this special community of practice.

The above vignette illustrates just one intangible element of how a class represents a shared community, as well as how pedagogy can be enacted in day-to-day classroom life. It also shows the need for teachers to be attentive to the conversations of the classroom. As we orchestrate classroom life, our pedagogy involves and indeed requires class members to communicate in varied ways as they enact lives together. Learning is occurring constantly, much of it not sanctioned or known by the teacher. Learning for life is occurring within the cut and thrust of daily classroom life. The sideways glances of one student to another, the note passed around the room, the secret use of social media, and so on, all communicate meaning from one to another. School life is filled with such communication between students participating simultaneously in varied communities of practice. And of course, the teacher is rarely a member of them. I will address student membership in multiple communities of practice in greater detail in chapter 6. Life has limitless intertextual[24] connections and barely visible meanings which are nevertheless known and understood by those who share specific practices, meanings, and textual histories.

Education requires the teacher to be attentive to the conversations of the classroom, the responses and attitudes of students, and the cultural practices evident in the words and actions of participants. But more than this, somehow we need to engage in their world as much as possible. No, not by pretending to be one of the students, but by building trusting relationships where the students have respect for their teachers and know they want what is good for them. Reflecting on and influencing the "communal intentions toward one another and the world"[25] in any classroom is critical work for the teacher. We have a responsibility to read the hearts and characters of our students in their actions and words, and accept our role in the

24. Intertextuality in simple terms refers to the juxtaposition and relationship of two or more texts. I wrote extensively about intertextuality in the 1980s and 1990s in relation to school language and literacy. Cairney, "Intertextuality," 478–84, and Cairney, *Pathways to Literacy*.

25. Dykstra, *Growing in the Life of Faith*, xi.

formation of students as we seek to direct them toward the good. This will require open and significant positive relationships with parents as well.[26]

The work of Douglas Barnes mentioned in earlier chapters, and that of Jerome Harste and his colleagues,[27] has helped me articulate two key understandings that have relevance to this book.[28] First, communication is central to learning and pedagogy, and second, learning needs to be enacted, not just encountered cognitively. In looking at the fundamental importance of communication to learning and curriculum, Barnes sought to get behind the taken-for-granted day-to-day activities of classrooms. In many ways, implicit in Barnes's work was a particular pedagogy (even though he used the word "curriculum" in its place). Barnes saw the classroom and the school as places where minds are not simply engaged, but rather curriculum and learning experiences are enacted. The moment-to-moment interactions in a classroom may at times have little to do with the mainstream curriculum, but they always have something to do with community life and shared community practices, whether situated within the class, specific sub-groups, or simply between two students.

Barnes saw such enactment[29] as involving the living out of learning as students communicated with one another in the places we call schools and classrooms. Classrooms and other school contexts are places where students don't simply learn the content of a curriculum, or only respond to the appropriate methods designed to teach; children learn as extensions of varied relationships. The above vignette about Phillip and the reading

---

26. It is beyond the scope of this book to consider some of my previous research and writing in home-school relationships, but many resources and publications can be found on my personal website: www.trevorcairney.com. You might also like to drop into the blog I write that is associated with this book. You can find it at http://pedagogyandformation.blogspot.com.au/.

27. Harste et al., *Language Stories and Literacy Lessons*.

28. See, for example, Cairney, "The Social Foundations of Literacy," and Cairney, *Pathways to Literacy*.

29. The term "enactment" has a legal dimension but it is used here to represent the way people act with regard to limitations and constraints they perceive in their world. Weick uses the term enactment to recognize that the actions of people in any context are always in relationship to other people. Any individual who acts in a group, such as a classroom, contributes to their own self-formation and that of the group. For example, individuals can enact limitations in any social context to avoid issues or experiences. This might involve not talking, refusing to answer questions, resisting specific practices or language, and so on. See Weick, "Cognitive Processes in Organization," 41–74.

of *Lester and Clyde* earlier in the chapter demonstrates how the school life orchestrated by the teacher matters, and it makes a difference.

Classrooms are places where children learn many things about the rules and norms of classroom and school life. For example, what is an appropriate response to the work of others? How might they humbly ask a question of someone else's work, or deal with their own (and others') success and failure? They will also learn how to relate to other learners in varied contexts, including the classroom and playground. Their learning also extends to how they fulfill varied relationship roles, including that of student, friend, academic rival, fellow believer, and so on. And of course, as my earlier example of Phillip suggests, this may even extend to how they deal with the annoying behavior of another member of the community.

Secular theorists and researchers like James Gee suggest what is happening to our students day by day is, in effect, a process of "being apprenticed to a social group,"[30] and of course he is correct. The way we behave, the meanings we derive, the things we compose or create, reflect who we are, what we have experienced, what we know about language and the world, and also our purposes for creating them in the first place.[31] Every act of discourse is in some sense a social construct of specific groups and offers limitless opportunities for learning and the shaping of ideas, attitudes, passions, and beliefs.

Barbara Rogoff helpfully expands on the metaphor of apprenticeship to describe how children learn and become part of school communities of practice. She suggests children are effectively apprenticed into thinking in certain ways. They are:

> active in their efforts to learn from observing and participating with peers and more skilled members of their society, developing skills to handle culturally defined problems.[32]

While Rogoff rightly places great emphasis on the actions of students on one another, the teacher has a critical role to play in leading his or her apprentices. As James Heap reminds us, through their actions, teachers signal what they see as appropriate, what roles are possible (and valued), how

---

30. Gee, *Social Linguistics and Literacies*, 52.

31. Cairney, *Pathways to Literacy*, 8.

32. Rogoff, *Apprenticeship in Thinking*, 7.

students are to take up these roles, and what counts as appropriate behavior, attitudes, values, and activities in the classroom.[33]

As well, Ana Heras suggests all classrooms have a range of "lived opportunities, possibilities, and constraints opened up . . . [and dependent] on the configurations made possible by the institutional organization of the school and classroom *and* by the social and academic interactions within these institutional spaces."[34] Hence, knowledge is always related to the opportunities students have to engage and interact with each other.

The various patterns of social action, discourse, and classroom activities sanctioned by the teacher and members of the class tend to lead to what Kris Gutierrez showed to be the formation of specific frameworks for classroom interaction that she called recitation "scripts."[35] My own research with Jean Ashton situated in families[36] showed that these consistent frameworks tended to lead to compliant adherence, and outcomes that are predictable and which place limits on the type of knowledge constructed and used.[37]

THE TEACHER'S ROLE IN SHAPING
LEARNING AND MEANING

In beginning to respond to and expand on my comments above, we need to consider more closely how the teacher is engaged in a process of forming communities of practice within classrooms. Rogoff's work[38] mentioned above is a helpful starting point. Central to her concept of being apprenticed in thinking is the work of Lev Vygotsky, who similarly has had a significant impact on my own research.

Vygotsky's[39] theoretical work suggested that higher-order processes like literacy and the other areas of knowledge for life can only be acquired through interaction with others before later being carried out independent-

---

33. Heap, "What Counts as Reading," 265–92.

34. Heras, "The Construction of Understanding in a Sixth-Grade Classroom," 276.

35. Gutierrez, "How Talk, Context and Script Shape Contexts for Learning," 335–65.

36. Cairney and Ashton, "Three Families, Multiple Discourses," 303–45.

37. The use of consistent scripts shapes contexts and hence conversations about specific topics. As well, they tend to limit opportunities for students to interact with and receive help from others, and to limit the teacher's opportunity to go beyond the superficial and at times scripted interactions of classroom life.

38. Rogoff, *Apprenticeship in Thinking.*

39. Vygotsky, *Mind in Society.*

ly. He argued that learning moves from an initial form of guided learning to independent learning. He suggested controversially that there are two developmental "levels," rather than a series of lockstep stages as proposed by Piaget.[40] The first stage Vygotsky termed "actual development," which he defined as "the level of development of a child's mental functions . . . determined by independent problem-solving."[41] In other words, what a child can do alone at a particular point in time. The second he called "potential development," defined as what a child can achieve if given the benefit of support during the task. This is the ability to solve problems "under adult guidance or in collaboration with more capable peers."[42]

Vygotsky suggested there is always a difference between these two forms of development, and the gap between them is the "zone of proximal development" (ZPD). This, he argued, indicates the functions that in effect have not matured, but are in the process of doing so. A key premise for him was that learning creates the zone of proximal development, and "awakens a variety of internal development processes that are able to operate only when the child is interacting with people in his environment and in cooperation with his peers. Once these processes are internalized, they become part of the child's independent developmental achievement."[43]

Vygotsky and others like Rogoff sought to interpret his work and argue that the ZPD is a dynamic region of sensitivity to learning the skills of culture, in which children develop through participation in problem-solving with more experienced members of a group.[44]

Vygotsky suggested that teaching geared toward developmental levels that have already been achieved will be ineffective, and that "the only 'good learning' is that in advance of development."[45] But how is this learning fostered, and what is our role in it as teachers? With the support of others more skilled and knowledgeable than the student. While Vygotsky was talking about cognitive learning and development, the work applies to

40. Dr. Jean Piaget was a giant in the field of psychology and had an enormous impact on education in the twentieth century. You can find a biographical overview at http://www.piaget.org/aboutPiaget.html.

41. Vygotsky, *Mind in Society*, 86.

42. Ibid., 86.

43. Ibid., 90.

44. Rogoff, *Apprenticeship in Thinking*.

45. Vygotsky, *Mind in Society*, 89.

learning in any area of life, including how to behave, how to participate in groups, how to deal with problems, and so on.

Jerome Bruner[46] devised the concept of scaffolding to explain the process. He described the act of scaffolding as a process whereby the teacher helped students by doing what the child could not do alone at first. The teacher's role was to control the focus of attention, demonstrate and segment the task, and so on.

Rogoff's contribution was to see this process of learning and the role of others in it, as guided participation. This is also useful in helping to explain how Vygotsky's views on learning can be put into practice in classrooms. She saw both guidance and participation as essential to children's development. This guidance can have varied forms, including tacit or explicit, and participation varying in "the extent to which children or caregivers are responsible for its arrangement."[47]

Central to the concept of guided participation is the concept of intersubjectivity. In broad terms, this refers to the relationship between people that involves shared focus and purpose, leading to meaning that requires social, cognitive, and emotional exchange with others. When such shared focus and purpose exists, we see intersubjectivity present whether language is used or not. Vygotsky suggests intersubjectivity provides both the basis for communication to occur and also potential support for the child to extend existing understanding to varied contexts and situations. As people interact in this open way, perspectives may be reshaped, and an understanding of the perspectives of others achieved.

What the above research demonstrates is classroom interaction has its own ability to shape the way students respond or remain silent, and even the types of responses that are expected and primed by the discourse practices common to teaching. Much of this is within the teacher's control as part of classroom practices, but much of it is not once our students step outside the formal activities of classroom life. Drawing on the work outlined above I want to look more closely at the relationship between learning and formation.

46. Bruner, *Child's Talk*, and Bruner, *Actual Minds, Possible Worlds*.
47. Rogoff, *Apprenticeship in Thinking*, 8.

LEARNING AND FORMATION

I have already suggested learning has traditionally been seen as mainly about cognition and activity of the mind, dependent primarily on a variety of skills. But of course, this is only half the story. Few definitions or discussions of learning recognize it is also a social and cultural practice, taking place as learners relate to one another. These relationships matter and play a part in what we eventually believe and know. Learning is very much a social and cultural process, not just a cognitive one. Bruner suggested that "culture and the quest for meaning within culture are the proper causes of human action," not simply skills, knowledge, and abilities. This sociocultural process is mediated by symbolic means with narrative playing a key role. Bruner argued that culture is the forum for induction through education. We prepare children for life as they partake in a forum for negotiating and renegotiating meaning that is part of any culture.[48]

Wenger, Vygotsky, Bruner, and Rogoff all suggest that members of communities negotiate meanings as they participate within them. Wenger takes this a little further by stressing we also ultimately agree on meanings and practices.[49] Our engagement in the world requires us to bring and negotiate meanings. This in turn requires members of groups to engage and participate in varied activities, sometimes resisting meanings and at other times accepting them. Sometimes we are initiators of meaning, and sometimes we respond to the meanings of others.

Wenger suggests that over time collective learning results in practices that reflect common pursuits or goals. Practices are rarely alone, and always sit within social and historical contexts that give structure and meaning to human action. Practices can be explicit and visible in the form of language, images, roles, procedures, and tools. But they can also be tacit in the form of "implicit relations," silent conventions, unspoken rules, intuitions, crafted sensitivities, or "embodied understandings."[50]

These varied practices ultimately lead to the shared formation of beliefs and actions that are seen as appropriate and acceptable within groups. The vignette discussed earlier in this chapter illustrates how this took place in one instance.

48. Bruner, *Actual Minds, Possible Worlds*, 123.

49. Wenger, *Communities of Practice*, 51–71.

50. Ibid., 45–49.

Wenger suggests that reification[51] gives form to our experience through objects that communicate or concentrate meaning. Reification, he suggests, occupies much of a group's collective energy and shapes our experience. Community life produces shared abstractions, tools, symbols, stories, terms, and concepts.[52] In institutions like schools, reification can come from outside the community (e.g., old boys, government policies, media, etc.). A principal or a teacher can reify community practices with inarticulate as well as articulate phrases, words, stances, behaviors, and objects. We have probably heard some of them before: "Boys in the first fifteen at this school never give in"[53]; "this school expects effort"; "parents are always welcome to discuss their child's progress"; "your parents don't pay your school fees to see you mess around."

Wenger reminds us that succinctness and the ability to focus community practice is also its greatest weakness. For the principal or teachers, words can quickly become hollow slogans that mask an unwillingness to understand the complexity of communities of practice and miss the point of member resistance, ambivalence, or hostility.

David Smith and James Smith offer a helpful reminder that Christian education is not just about convincing children of Christian ideas, or even "assent to a set of propositions."[54] They cite Craig Dykstra and Dorothy Bass, who argue for a view of education that places a priority on the church as a community of practice. Indeed, they suggest it is much more than this, as has been argued throughout this book. As Dykstra stresses, "The life of the Christian faith is the practice of many practices."[55] I will return to this significant work in chapter 6, as I begin to outline in greater detail what I am recommending for teachers in terms of a practical pedagogy for life within the school community.

51. At its base, reification means to make or treat an abstraction as real or existing, or to make something immaterial become concrete. Wenger defines reification more generally as "the process of giving form to our experience." In 1972, in Australia, one of the major political parties managed to reify how the majority of the voters felt about the nation. The slogan "It's Time" became the chant that reflected a generation's sense that things weren't right and progressive change was essential. Practices, views, prejudices, hopes, and experiences can become reified, and in a sense, make real and more tangible that which is abstract and immaterial.

52. Ibid., 58–61.

53. For people unfamiliar with the sport of rugby, it is a tough contact sport played with teams of fifteen players in many elite secondary schools in Australia and Britain.

54. David Smith and James Smith, *Teaching and Christian Practices*, 14.

55. Dykstra, *Growing in the Life of Faith*, 67.

HABIT, TELOS AND COMMUNITY LIFE

My argument in this book is the education of our students requires the teacher's orchestration of the life of the classroom in the shaping of student character. Merely instrumentalizing a practice in order to satisfy some other external end is not likely to lead to a change in character or long-term behavior or belief. Our students are masters at complying with the practices of school when it is necessary, but of course this is not formation.

The concept of habit is foundational to much of the discussion in this chapter, for it goes to the heart of what it might mean for children to be changed in character. In the more recent discussions of habit, the work of Pierre Bourdieu and his theoretical work on "habitus," has been discussed widely in educational and sociological literature.[56] What Bourdieu's work focuses on is the interplay of agency, that is the power of the individual to make choices and act independently, and structure the way things are arranged in their world to restrain or limit choices. His work also has a strong relationship to power and how it is distributed and limited within social groups.

Bourdieu argued that cultural practices of varied kinds are embodied, not just matters of the mind. The very culture of groups and communities is present in the actions, words, and values of people. We accept and take these on as part of our membership of groups. This occurs primarily through what Bourdieu calls habitus, which describes socialized norms or tendencies that guide behavior and thinking. Habitus defines and represents the rules, values, norms, beliefs, and practices of a group. He saw these as "deposited" in us as we engage in communities.[57]

Bourdieu developed a social theory to explain how we learn the rules of discourse. He argued that over time, specific communities have members who take on particular habits, dispositions, actions, preferences, and even beliefs. These become embodied in the life of the community.[58] The habitus shapes the responses of group members to the unpredictable events within community life and gives form to daily life.

When Jackie, whom we met in Vignette 1 (see chapter 2), moved from one community of practice to another, she was entering and being immersed in a different habitus, which placed different constraints on her

---

56. Bourdieu, *Outline of a Theory of Practice*.

57. Ibid., 170.

58. Ibid., 170–75.

as well as new expectations. And of course each habitus also had a different *telos* and carried with it different ways of behaving, different priorities for action, and even different expectations about interaction and behavior. The cultural and subcultural dispositions of members of Jackie's various groups (or communities of practice, to use Wenger's phrase), were actually embodied within the members of the group. This is the challenge for any teacher or school principal. While we can control how our students might act in sanctioned school activities, what they do on the bus, in public, with friends after hours, on excursions, and in the playground is something out of our control as they move from one habitus to another.

The following more personal vignette might enable me to clarify what I think Wenger means by this.

Vignette 6: Removing "Basinning" at a University Residential College

When I was appointed as Master of a residential college in 2002 within a secular university, I encountered a couple of community practices that seemed totally out of place in today's society. One of these was a practice called "basinning." This involved a number of members of the community grabbing an individual and carrying them to a bathroom or source of water, holding them down, and splashing them with warm and cold water scooped from hand basins. This practice continued until they were drenched or until their protests became more strident. The victims sounded reluctant, but never complained afterwards and seemed to accept it. It tended to occur on their birthdays, when they had done something silly or inappropriate, or for reasons unclear to everyone.

The practice seemed to me to be completely out of place in the twenty-first century. It also seemed to have the potential to lead to injury, abuse of power, damage to facilities and property, and so on. I decided the practice needed to stop. I notified the members of the community that I was considering banning the practice and outlined my reasons for doing so. I sat down first with the student leaders, and called a public meeting for interested community members to discuss my proposed action and to hear their views. A meeting was held that was attended by more than fifty relatively hostile people (which was 25 percent of the residents at the time).

After about ninety minutes the conversation had run its course. It was clear that there were varied views. Some (a minority) had reluctantly agreed that it needed to be banned, some were hostile in their opposition, and others simply wanted to hang on to this cultural practice and ignore the arguments. What was fascinating was that throughout the meeting, people stressed that basinning was: an important part of community life, important for community cohesiveness and membership, vital to building group identity, critical in the early weeks of each year to help people to get to know one another, and not easily replaced with anything else.

I banned the practice a week later and experienced a degree of hostility and subtle resistance from sectors of the community for at least two years. Later, I was to reflect on the above incident and conclude a number of things. First, the practice, even though inappropriate, was certainly an important part of community life, and had been reified in this community as a key cultural practice that bound members of the community together. It was seen as vital to how this remarkable group of talented, close, and supportive people formed community. Second, while the practice had many problems and needed to be stopped, it was a critical way in which groups incorporated new members, and excluded or disciplined others toward compliance with group norms. Third, basinning was one of the things that marked membership of the group and gave tangible expression to it. It was such a close community, that members could drag one of its own to the bathroom and drench them to show that they were part of a close-knit group, and this was broadly accepted, hence the absence of complaints that made their way to my office or even my residential staff.

This obscure practice within my college illustrates Wenger's point that the negotiation of meaning within communities of practice involves the convergence of participation and reification. When these come together effectively, they exercise control over the community's accepted meanings and can give stability. I disrupted this, it was complied with, but it took time for my intervention to be accepted.

My actions in banning basinning were probably seen as the action of an "outsider,"[59] as it threatened stability and the distribution of power. Wenger suggests that such control and power within any community of

59. Pierre Bourdieu's distinction between synoptic and participatory viewpoints has relevance here. Synoptic views stand outside any enactment of a practice (viewed retrospectively), whereas participatory views examine the practice or action as a participant, not a retrospective observer. My response was shaped as an observer, whereas in time, as I became an insider (albeit, one with a unique position of power), who was seen increasingly this way, I was able to understand the practice differently. In retrospect, if I had dealt with it as a participant rather than as an outsider, I may have handled the removal of the practice differently. See Bourdieu, *Outline of a Theory of Practice*, and Bourdieu, *The Logic of Practice*, for further discussion of this distinction.

practice must be constantly "reproduced, reasserted, [and] renegotiated in practice."[60] Again, James Smith's concept of "secular liturgy" is relevant here. It is important to stress that ideas are implicated in the exercise of power, but these are demonstrated in practice. Basinning had become a "formative practice" (or liturgy)[61] that helped to shape the resident views of what it meant to be a member of this community, and what was vital to maintaining the close relationships that were the glue that held this together. This of course reinforces the arguments of James Smith[62] and Craig Dykstra[63] that secular liturgies and practices have a powerful role in shaping communities. The residents were part of a unique habitus that had shaped not only the ideas about what constitutes community, but also their embodied actions as part of it. But also, the reverse was in operation because as members began to comply with practices, they had a role to play in shaping the ideas that justified the practice.

This of course reflects the power of community and the influence of the many overlapping communities of practice in everyday life that shape us. Within my college, the habitus that we see evident in the basinning practices had constrained, or perhaps persuaded, intelligent young women, confident and assertive in their personal lives, to allow five or six big guys to drag them into a bathroom and drench them with water. Furthermore, they were prepared to see this as an important and natural community practice. This idea seems absurd, and yet the practice had become reified as a mark of the strength of community life.

I want to conclude this chapter by outlining six principles for learning which I hope are transparent. These reflect my argument about the way meaning is negotiated and constructed, the role the teacher plays in meaning-making within school and classroom life, and finally, the formative nature of classroom life and how teachers exercise influence upon it.

First, learning takes place within a web of relationships, or perhaps multiple webs of relationships. This includes relationships between teachers and students, parents and teachers, and among students themselves.

Second, learners have membership in multiple communities of practice that they inhabit concurrently.

---

60. Wenger, *Communities of Practice*, 93.

61. Smith, *Desiring the Kingdom*, 24–25.

62. Ibid., 85–88.

63. Dykstra, *Growing in the Life of Faith*, 66–78.

Third, learners help shape, and in turn are shaped by, communities of practice and learning occurs within the messy and disengaged moments of life.

Fourth, learners are part of the process of establishing rules, expectations, and shared beliefs in communities, as members negotiate meanings and participate within others and ultimately reify particular meanings and practices. Our engagement in the world requires us to bring and negotiate meanings as we engage and participate in varied practices.

Fifth, learners and learning are always influenced by a *telos*, or end goal. A common thread that runs through many of the discussions of cultural practices and community life is a recognition of language, narrative, and meaning. As James Smith has suggested, members of communities of practice like my college, and of course our schools, have their imaginations captured through the stories and practices of life. This can occur, he suggested, through what he calls "secular liturgies."[64] Related to this, I will consider the power of story in chapter 7, and the role of imagination in chapter 8.

Sixth, power is implicated in learning and the practices of learners. No discussion of practice within institutions like schools can ignore power. My discussion of basinning demonstrates a number of issues in relation to power, and the practice of many practices, and how this occurs within community life. This will be picked up in more detail in chapter 6, as will the way children are formed within the life of the school.

64. James Smith, *Erotic Comprehension*, 5.

PART II

Education and Life

6

Classroom Life

Every activity, every enquiry, every practice aims at some good; for by "the good" or "a good" we mean that at which human beings characteristically aim.[1]

—ALASDAIR MACINTYRE

The metaphor of the teacher as a guide includes both direction by the teacher and active involvement of the student in the learning process.[2]

—DANIEL J. ESTES

The second half of this book shifts from considering the nature of education and the theoretical and biblical arguments for an authentic transformative pedagogy, to the application and use of this pedagogy in the school and classroom. It is framed by a single question: How might teachers fulfill their roles in relation to the formation of children who inhabit multiple communities of practice in a world of competing stories and visions of the good life? As I outlined in chapter 1, this book has been shaped by my definition of education, which is that, "education is the whole of life of a community and the experience of its members learning to live this life from a specific standpoint or end goal." In the second half of the book, I explore how we

1. MacIntyre, *After Virtue*, 148.
2. Estes, *Hear, My Son*, 130.

85

might support, teach, equip, and guide our students as they navigate varied communities of practice within and outside the classroom.

A DIFFERENT FOCUS FOR TEACHERS

In earlier chapters I have offered a biblical and educational justification for my argument that if we want to offer education worthy of the label "Christian," we need a renewed emphasis on pedagogy. I have also stressed that by "pedagogy" I mean the way the life of the classroom is shaped by the teacher with the participation of all others. I have covered much ground, but as I concluded chapter 5 I outlined the fundamental planks that underpin my conception of pedagogy. The view of pedagogy outlined in this book defines learning as an activity socially constituted within communities of practice, not simply classrooms and schools. Learning takes place within the life of the many communities in which students and teachers participate. As they live within the places we call schools, they are shaped and given direction and focus by communicated (and absorbed) goals, desires, and shared beliefs. As teachers, we are doing much more than imparting knowledge and skills; we are also forming young lives as we engage with them in a rich life of apprenticeship, mentoring, and discipleship.

I have suggested that Christian pedagogy will lead to an education that points toward kingdom goals in the moment-to-moment life of the classroom. It is not simply the delivery of doctrine and teaching in chapel, Scripture classes, and Bible studies, nor is it simply the reinforcement of a specific worldview. Pedagogy will always reflect the attitudes of the teacher, the purposes that drive classroom activities, discipline and praise, rewards and punishment, as well as the words spoken and the knowledge shared. This is an education that is implicitly, and sometimes explicitly, centered on God's purposes for his creatures, not simply the pursuit of the goals of the world.

I have argued that at times in the past, what the church has offered in the name of education for our children has been undermined by the pursuit of end goals that have been based on an assumption that simply seeks to fill children's heads with ideas, values, and right knowledge; this is not enough for transformation to occur.[3] Our hope as Christian teachers is surely that biblical teaching and insights will be associated with a change in children's hearts, but of course the mere transmission of knowledge will not

---

3. Cairney et al., *New Perspectives in Anglican Education.*

achieve this outcome. The transformation of the heart requires the work of the Spirit in the lives of our children. The teacher has a key role to play in this as they feed, structure, and support a classroom life that encourages children to ask questions of the teacher and one another as they search for answers to life's greatest needs like love, acceptance, forgiveness, and hope. This will occur in communities of trust, where they can grow in confidence and knowledge of their God and their hoped-for future. All of this occurs in an environment that assists them in making sense of the conflicting messages they encounter across the many communities of practices in which they participate.

Whether we are educating children as parents, schoolteachers, clergy, or Sunday school teachers, we need to create contexts in which children are taught clearly about God and his purposes, and urge them to see how his goals for them make sense within their lives. This requires a clear understanding of the ends to which we want to direct children, and the need to offer narratives and teaching that challenge and connect with them. I say more about the power of story in chapter 7, but what I am getting at here is children need to be able to connect the biblical story of sin, estrangement from God, redemption, salvation, judgment, and resurrection with their own lives, not simply the heroes or failures we read in the Bible.

To push my point just a little more, a Bible story, for example, needs to be told in such a way that it acknowledges key biblical themes. For example, the story of Samson, which we find in the book of Judges,[4] is a story about a man born as a Nazirite—that is, someone separated or set aside for God. But this chosen man ignored his Nazirite vow of devotion to God and was distracted by the beauty of Delilah, and hence he sinned. When the Philistines threatened Judah, he trusted in his strength and ability to save the day, rather than his God. He then succumbed to the guile of Delilah. Though Samson was born with the potential to serve God and honor him, in his weakness he fails. This is not a story about a strong man having his hair cut causing him to lose strength. Rather, it is a story about disobedience, trust, and God's deliverance and mercy. Connecting such a story to young children's lives is what matters and is needed when the Bible is taught. This is not just a curious and riveting ancient story for children's entertainment. No, it is to be used to encourage them to use it as a mirror to see how they too can be delivered from disobedience and learn to trust their God. We need to engage with our students at a level beyond access to the literal

4. Judg 13–18.

level of what they know or are prepared to share with us. We need to move beyond the language of curriculum to language and interaction centered on life!

A key tool within our pedagogical toolbox will be the ability to ask the right questions. Questioning as a pedagogical tool has its roots in Socratic teaching. As Hyman suggests, to think of teaching without questions is impossible.[5] I've written extensively about the use of questions as part of pedagogy, because how we ask questions of our students, how we listen to their responses, and how we act upon what we hear and see matters![6] As I have argued elsewhere, the development of taxonomies of questions from 1950 to 1980 shone a light on the possibilities as well as the problems with questioning. Taxonomies like those developed by Benjamin Bloom still have a place,[7] but the problem with questioning has been that many teachers see a direct relationship between the type, frequency, rate, and timing of our questions.[8] More important considerations are whether teachers listen and watch their students before asking questions. Not asking a particular question at a particular time is just as important as asking the right question at the right time. The true art of asking questions commences with deep knowledge of your children, listening ears and hearts that seek their good. In many ways, the most basic tool in the teacher's toolkit is the art of the open personal question: Why did you say that? How does this make you feel? Why did you react like that? Are you okay? What's troubling you? Why is this stressing you so much? Why are you so quiet today? Is there a reason you never remember your homework? Questions of this type do much more than gain a quick answer to a procedural or a curriculum topic. While the latter specific questions matter too, the open questions allow greater access to the hearts of our students: their interests, life outside school, and the things that trouble, frustrate, and excite them. This type of question offers a window into their loves and desires.

Our classrooms need to be places where our children listen and apply biblical teaching to their lives. While for the two-year-old and the

---

5. Hyman, *Strategic Questioning*, 8.

6. See, for example, Cairney, *Teaching Reading Comprehension*, 28–36; Cairney, *Pathways to Literacy*, 40–47. As well, you can visit the blog dedicated to this book at http://pedagogyandformation.blogspot.com.au/.

7. Anderson and Krathwohl, *A Taxonomy for Learning, Teaching, and Assessing.* You can download an introduction by Krathwohl. See http://rt3region7.ncdpi.wikispaces.net/file/view/8+Perspectives+on+RBT.pdf.

8. See Cairney, *Pathways to Literacy*, 40–47.

thirteen-year-old, this will require varied forms of engagement, all contexts for learning require strong relationships of trust and openness with the "tellers," that is, the key adults in their lives. As well, they need an informed understanding of how they can do likewise with their peers. In this way, our children will be open to connecting the story of their lives with the hope of the Christian gospel.

The first half of the book has taken us across varied territory, including consideration of biblical wisdom in relation to teaching, education, and Christian formation, and its relationship to the best of educational, philosophical, anthropological, sociological, and psychological literature. All of this has been explored as a foundation to understanding our roles as teachers in communities of practice where children gain faith and have it tested. At this point, we ask how might we reconcile biblical understanding with what we have learned about the nature of learning, personhood, the social foundations of life, and the role that multiple communities of practice play in the shaping of desire and one's view of the good life? My conclusion is schools, churches, and Christian families need to spend more time considering the ways they help, support, and direct their children, in order to focus lives toward goals that have eternal significance. We need a pedagogy consistent with our goals of Christian formation.

The challenge is for Christian teachers and schools to see a right place for the common goals of schooling within pedagogical practices for our in-between lives. As I reminded readers in chapter 1, we are called to lead lives that are pleasing to God and consistent with his purposes; we are in a biblical sense "strangers and aliens" in this world (1 Pet 1:16–18). While God made us to live in the world, it is very much an in-between existence for Christians. The challenge is not to be so focused on the achievements of the world that we lose sight of the biblical call to fix our sights on our future eternal existence with Christ. Christian schools can at times seem as if their aims and priorities are fixed firmly on worldly achievements and success. Our aim must be to create environments that prioritize an integrated faith-directed and gospel-focused life! Our pedagogy is to be one that supports the formation of children who we cannot assume share this view of the world. Our hope is that as they live their school lives in Christ-centered schools, they will begin to understand what it means to follow Jesus and the priorities this brings for our lives.

I argued in chapter 5 that our goal as Christian teachers is to shift our students from a focus on the desires of the world to a *telos* that focuses on different end goals. Alasdair MacIntyre has probably done more than any other writer to clarify what this means. Using virtue as a key category he argues for a shift in attention away from a Thomist[9] view of the world that argues for the teaching of wisdom, and instead points to the role of social practices in formation.[10] He suggests that good habits focused on an ultimate "good" and character are born in the crucible of daily "practices." He defines practices as "any coherent and complex form of socially established cooperative human activity through which goods internal to that form of activity are realized in the course of trying to achieve those standards of excellence, and are appropriate to, and partially definitive of, that form of activity."[11] MacIntyre believes the result of such practices is the achievement of excellence and the extension of human goods. Such practices should have internal as well as external goods.

An important extension of what MacIntyre argues is that while we can teach children to memorize a catechism and reward them for doing so, unless they are able to internalize the goods to which the catechism points, they will fail to embrace the practice in any deep sense. If so, we have failed to have a transformational influence on their lives. Herein lies our greatest challenge as Christian teachers; how do we create contexts for learning where practices communicate internal and external goods, and hence teach and model the truth of God pointing our children to eternal goals not just earthly ones?

I have already suggested in earlier discussions that in adopting such a pedagogy we do not need to reject the goals that seem to be the primary focus of many of our schools, including excellence, skill, effort, success, and so on. Rather, we need to reposition the use of these things for God's glory, not our own and that of the school. We need a pedagogy that demonstrates a clear understanding of the goals that matter most to God, and

---

9. Thomist conceptions of education see the central aim of education as a search for truth and wisdom. It is founded in the work of Thomas Aquinas who argued that while skills and scientific knowledge are important, the getting of wisdom must be our chief aim. The problem with Thomism is wisdom can often be presented as content to be learned, rather than teaching that transforms.

10. There isn't space to discuss MacIntyre's ideas on virtue here, but I need to stress that like values and worldview, the embracing of a virtues-based approach to schooling runs the risk that one set of rational and intellectual categories to be taught to children will be replaced by another with little connection to the good. Alasdair MacIntyre of course understands this, and argues that any embracing of a virtues-based approach must be situated under a biblical *telos*. That is, we should speak of virtues only when one has a clear teleology in mind. He has much to say about this. See MacIntyre, *After Virtue*.

11. Ibid., 187.

which place all other goals in their proper place subordinate to his goals; but more on this later.

FORMATION AS THE OUTCOME OF THE "PRACTICE OF MANY PRACTICES"

As I indicated in chapter 5, I have benefitted from the wisdom of Craig Dykstra and Dorothy Bass. In their work, they rightly stress the need for educators to create opportunities that bring to "consciousness the hidden dimensions embedded in and through our actions and relations and institutions."[12] This has strong resonance with my own emphasis on the social construction of communities of practice, the importance of deep relationships between teachers and their children, and the impact of the moment-to-moment life of classrooms.

While I'm grateful for the clarity of the work of Dykstra and Bass, much of their primary work has been applied to education in the church, and also in church-based Christian schools. These are typically sites where there has been a strong and accepted central faith commitment from teachers, parents, and students. While there are Christian schools of this type within Australia, many schools set up by the church demonstrate far less agreement among the teachers, parents, and students concerning the central purpose of the school and the foundational place of faith. This means the predominant emphasis on Christian practices by Dykstra and Bass as the primary vehicle for transformation may not be the most effective or viable strategy in all "Christian" schools. Dykstra and Bass define Christian practices as

> the things Christian people do together over time to address fundamental human needs in response to and in light of God's active presence for the life of the world.[13]

I like this definition. It is one I can work with and in one sense embrace. However, the central approach I am exploring in this book is not so much where Dykstra and Bass end up, that is, identifying and replicating Christian practices within life. Instead, my focus in on how Christian teachers and schools help students to see, respond to, and navigate all of the practices of life (Christian and non-Christian), with a *telos* that is shaped

---

12. Dykstra, *Growing in the Life of Faith*, xii.

13. Dykstra and Bass, "A Theological Understanding of Christian Practices," 6.

by and directed toward the kingdom of God. Many of our students in Christians schools are not in fact Christians at all, so they are on a journey toward an understanding of how Christians might respond in specific situations. This discussion relates back to my comments in chapter 3, when I discussed what life might look like in these in-between times. In most cases, our students are still on a journey toward faith, or rejection of it. This understanding should shift the focus of the Christian teacher and school. If so, I believe it will lead to better responses and practices that will help our students to deal with all of life's situations as they decide how to respond to the experiences and practices of their world.

My hope is we can challenge and support the emergence of our student views of the world, hopefully undergirded by an emerging, growing or existing faith. Such a focus is necessary in the broad educational contexts that I find of interest. However, I am not yet convinced that by "naturalizing Christian practices," Dykstra and Bass persuade me to accept their view that Christian practices are "unique" and should be our focal strategy.[14]

If our aim is to challenge and support the emergence of different views of the world—hopefully undergirded by emerging or existing faith—then we need to consider how this might occur. Of relevance in doing this is the role of habit discussed in chapter 5. This is an important consideration in light of Etienne Wenger's arguments about communities of practice. It is also critical to the major thesis of this book that pedagogy should be a central concern of teachers who are concerned with character formation. Habit is widely recognized as a key element of thought and action. But does it play a part in the moral and social development of our students and their formation as citizens, friends, team members, family members, and eventually employees, partners, and so on? And, if it does, how does this take place? As Tom Sparrow and Adam Hutchinson suggest, the "virtuous person is not defined by the skills she possesses, but by the habits she embodies and, with a certain virtuosity, summons in the appropriate circumstances."[15] They suggest an important question in light of this is, "Do habits constitute our first or second nature?"[16]

David Smith and James Smith make a significant contribution to our understanding of the question posed by Sparrow and Hutchinson.[17] In

---

14. David Smith and James Smith, *Teaching and Christian Practices*, 14–15.

15. Sparrow and Hutchinson, *A History of Habit*, 7.

16. Ibid., 2.

17. David Smith and James Smith, *Teaching and Christian Practices*.

seeking to clarify what we might mean by Christian practices, they argue focusing on Christian ideas, as Dykstra and Bass do, is not the way to proceed. I agree with this view regardless of whether by this we might mean virtues, values, or even worldview theory.[18] If ideas become the focus of our pedagogy, then the prospect of habits constituting a second nature, rather than simply compliant practices, will not be realized.

What Smith and Smith do with the Dykstra and Bass ideas on practices is to identify rightly that Christian practices have the potential to do much more than impact "the spiritual," they have the potential to "inscribe in us a habitus that primes and shapes our action." This, they conclude, has the potential to "configure how we see and act in the world."[19]

In recognizing the potential that a reframed idea of Christian practices might offer us to think about pedagogy in Christian colleges and universities, Smith and Smith suggest that a more formative approach such as MacIntyre's needs to be adopted (this was also explored in chapter 1).[20] In doing this, they seek to consider the relationship between specific Christian practices and settings for learning. Members of communities of practice like New College,[21] which is part of my immediate experience, and of course Christian schools everywhere, have their imaginations captured through the stories and practices of life. James Smith suggests this occurs through what he calls "secular liturgies."[22] He argues that participation in such liturgies over time helps to shape not just behavior, but what it means to belong to the group of people and the shared practices, dispositions, desires, and preferences of those who live in this place. I agree with this innovative approach as one way forward, but my task in this book is to present an approach to pedagogy that is not tied to the use of specific liturgical practices within our classrooms. Of course, I do see these at work day by day in our schools, and accept that they might well be a way forward in specific contexts for some of our students. Like James Smith, I agree that

18. I will probably be criticized for saying so little about worldview. This is not because I don't agree with worldview theory as an area of investigation. I simply don't believe a central focus on curriculum and teaching, based on analysis and critique of worldview and its relationship to classroom and curriculum practices, will take us far enough.

19. David Smith and James Smith, introduction to *Teaching and Christian Practices*, 15.

20. Ibid., 16.

21. New College is an Anglican college affiliated with the University of New South Wales Australia in Sydney. I was Master of this college from 2002 to 2016.

22. James Smith, "Erotic Comprehension," 5–6.

Christian formation is not about equipping knowers, but rather the formation of doers.[23]

As I have already mentioned in chapter 1, James Smith and his colleague David Smith have helpfully considered varied interpretations of what Christian practices might look like in a classroom.[24] In doing so, they take a significant lead from Craig Dykstra's argument that "the life of Christian faith is the practice of many practices."[25] Dykstra argues along with MacIntyre that specific practices have formative power. MacIntyre's definition of practice is narrower in its intent than that which Etienne Wenger would support, and this is reflected in the suggestion of Dykstra and Bass that Christian practices are "things Christian people do together over time in response to and in the light of God's active presence for the life of the world."[26]

I like the Dykstra and Bass definition a great deal, and it sits comfortably with my own thoughts on pedagogy. As well, I see in the related work that Dykstra and Bass have developed since the earlier definition that their emphasis is on the development of the richness of life of any community. It is in such contexts that God shapes us. Dykstra and Bass suggest that we need to learn to live this life in a specific context.[27] Their response, like mine, is to challenge teachers to engage in practices that are transformative.

However, as I stressed in chapter 5, the lives of our children are being enacted in an unregenerate state, surrounded by children at various stages in their walk toward faith in God, or at times, away from him. As well, with the backdrop of my comments on the diverse array of communities of practice in which they participate, I see limits to how effective we can be in maintaining the tight application of the Dykstra and Bass work if we place most of our emphasis on the use of specific practices and liturgies to shape our children.

David Smith and James Smith follow the Dykstra and Bass definition of practice in their attempt to examine what a Christian pedagogy might look like in classrooms.[28] Their choice makes sense when working primarily within a Christian theological college or perhaps senior Christian sec-

---

23. Ibid., 6.

24. David Smith and James Smith, *Teaching and Christian Practices*, 15–17.

25. Dykstra, *Growing in the Life of Faith,* 67.

26. Dykstra and Bass, "Times of Yearning, Practices of Faith," 5.

27. Ibid., 5.

28. David Smith and James Smith, *Teaching and Christian Practices*, 15–17.

ondary schools as they have been doing, but this direction will only take us so far in the preschool years and within primary schools. They argue that "Christian practices offer a kind of pedagogical wisdom that could reshape and redirect our classroom choices and strategies in surprising yet fruitful ways."[29]

Smith and Smith quite rightly expose the failure of Christians to give much thought to pedagogy at all. They suggest that even when they do, the focus is often on the content of what is taught, personal character, epistemology, and theology. Faith and learning, they argue, have been left behind.[30] In order to explore alternative approaches, they tested their ideas on educational practice in the classrooms of a group of teachers who undertook a course with them at Calvin College. They then encouraged their students to implement change in their own teaching contexts.

The teachers undertaking theological study with them were asked to design an intervention based on one or more Christian practices to apply in their teaching contexts. Each teacher was tasked to give an account of the connections between their Christian practices and their teaching and they did this in varied ways. For example, one teacher looked at testimony, fellowship, and hospitality and used these categories to bring about change in a course on adolescent psychology. Another implemented a shared meal out of class in the hope of enriching classroom engagement and relationships among students. A third modified course content and challenged first-year Liberal Arts students to consider how different life would be if led from the perspective of pilgrim, rather than that idea that of one with a "tourist gaze."[31] The intent of the project was to change the practices of teachers at the secondary and tertiary levels by challenging them to consider their practices within classrooms, and to strive to ensure that the students they taught could gain internal and external goods, and hence be transformed by what they were learning.

For Smith and Smith, as with Dykstra from whom they take their lead, the focus is on specific liturgies and practices. However, my focus is on the type of community that is created, the daily life that is evident, the practices that characterize it, and the impact these have on Christian formation. Of course, designing specific liturgies and practices, and a focus on developing

29. Ibid., 6.

30. Ibid., 3–7.

31. For their course content David Smith and James Smith drew on the work of Urry, *The Tourist Gaze*, 1–3.

community are not mutually exclusive. This is something with which Smith and Smith, as well as Dykstra, would agree, as they recognize both in their writing. As well, I want to stress that Smith and Smith and Dykstra share my belief that it is not the practice itself that changes anyone. As Dykstra states in quoting Dietrich Bonhoeffer's *Life Together*, it was not simply the act of reading the Bible in the midst of the holocaust that might have changed someone (although I should add that it can be if God so wills), but the reading of it in the "midst of providing care and hospitality to strangers while resisting powers that destroy."[32] In essence, he argues for engagement in Christian practices in the midst of life in all of its complexity and messiness.

Dykstra sees Christian practices as "habituations of the Spirit." He states,

> They are not, finally, activities we do to make something spiritual happen in our lives. Nor are they duties we undertake to be obedient to God. Rather, they are patterns of communal action that create openings in our lives where the grace, mercy, and presence of God may be made known to us. They are places where the power of God is experienced. In the end, these are not ultimately our practices but forms of participation in the practice of God.[33]

My view on this is that while the mere act of repeated engagement in a practice can be used by God to reveal himself to his people, God's revelation is rarely on the basis of repetitive habitual practices. While praying the Lord's Prayer each day, giving thanks to God for our food at mealtime, learning simple creeds, and adhering to varied practices are capable of speaking of the wisdom and purposes of God, our children often fail to engage with them in this way. They have not truly been habituated. Habituation is not merely a set of repeated behaviors. My own conversion that I will share in chapter 7 demonstrates what I mean. In my early life, I fled the imposition of any Christian practices in my home, school, or the church. While there is a clear place for life liturgies and Christian practices in schools, I believe that if this is our focus Christian education will drift toward a focus on curriculum and learning activities via another route, and perhaps by another name.[34]

32. Dykstra, *Growing in the Life of Faith*, 56.

33. Ibid., 66.

34. Similarly, I believe if we adopt the Dykstra and Bass definition of practice as they outline it, teachers will most likely end up advocating specific curriculum and methodological practices as the key. That is, curriculum by another name.

My belief is the power is not in the practice, or the teacher's ability to present the practice and engage students in it, but rather in the ability of the teacher to orchestrate the life of the classroom and the engagement of their students in the practice of many practices, as well as reflection on what this lived experience means.

My argument throughout this book is that much more foundational changes are required for communities of practice to become truly transforming. In the cut and thrust of complex classroom life, teachers will typically resort to what they know, the safety of curriculum, and varied methodological practices that are more structured and can more easily be tested to see if they work. Methods and curriculum approaches that are more prescriptive, predictable, and easy to plan, will always appear attractive to teachers when faced with classroom complexity. But the problem we face is, will such predictable and perhaps easier-to-replicate approaches prove transformative?

MacIntyre has been critical of teaching on the grounds that it "lacks its own internal good to serve as its telos."[35] He suggests teaching can simply serve a variety of goods reflecting the subjects and ideas being taught at the time.[36] My view is there is a very real risk that if we center our pedagogy on Christian practices we might end up doing nothing more than teaching Christian practices as a curriculum.[37]

If teachers end up doing this, my question is: Might the successful demonstration of a practice, if inserted into classroom life as a deliberate strategy, potentially lack an authentic internal good? In other words, might the modeling and application of a specific Christian practice (e.g., taking turns in class discussion and listening respectfully to the views of others), end up as no more than the demonstration of a practice to gain the approval of the teacher and others? And if so, how confident can we be that this will in any way be transformative once the curriculum context of these conversations is removed and our students face other contexts such as the playground? Finally, how likely is it that this practice will become second nature rather than mimicked practice?

---

35. MacIntyre and Dunne, "Alasdair MacIntyre on Education," 1–19.

36. David Smith and James Smith draw on Bourdieu's suggestion that practice can have its own logic, and put MacIntyre's criticism to one side, citing their lack of interest in what they see as MacIntyre's debate about "the status of the act of teaching." I don't see it as simply this and wish to engage with the issue.

37. Ibid., 10.

To understand fully what I am suggesting, a brief return to a discussion of Pierre Bourdieu's work is necessary. Bourdieu argued that knowledge is constructed and absorbed through practices within communities. His concept of habitus, which we discussed, earlier is critical to understanding the socialized norms or tendencies that guide behavior and thinking. Habitus is helpful in understanding why groups accept specific ways of acting and thinking and rules for association.

As we have already discussed, habitus is learned through practice within communities and is a type of embodied knowledge that Bourdieu suggests is internalized as a "second nature" as practice begins to have a logic of its own.[38] Group members begin to develop a specific structure of mind that has its own tastes, views, disposition, schemata for describing and making sense of reality, preferences, and so on. Status, power, and the relationships between group members are culturally and even symbolically established. Members make choices and decisions, and enact them within their lives.

For Bourdieu, habitus is created unconsciously within the everydayness of community life, without group members necessarily demonstrating any "deliberate pursuit of coherence."[39] This last point is important. Bourdieu is speaking of practices embedded within life communities, and largely invisible to participants, these are the practices that teachers need to understand, and to some extent shape and use for the good. Our schools are filled with students who suffer, resist, and tolerate the deliberate and obvious actions and Christian practices of teachers designed to point them towards Christ. It is here that my concerns with more systematic approaches to training or modeling Christian practices lies. This is not to deny that God can work through our shallow compliance, or in spite of our resistance and even rebellion, but the primary work of the teacher within communities needs to be in orchestrating life while curriculum is taught and character shaped.

Bourdieu's concept of habitus is powerful and helps us understand why as teachers we can share the same message over and over again with little impact on our students. It also helps us understand why students at times can give us the answers we want to hear, and yet fail to demonstrate this has had any impact on their life as they move in and out of varied communities of practice. It is why a group of intelligent young men and

38. Bourdieu, *The Logic of Practice*, 52–56.
39. Bourdieu, *Distinction*, 170.

women can embrace the practice of basinning (described in chapter 5) as a legitimate community practice while living within the community, but can look back on it five to ten years later after they have left, and be amazed that they would have accepted it at the time.

BEING SHAPED BY THAT WHICH IS INVISIBLE

In contrast to the approaches advocated by many Christian educators, I have suggested that teachers need to be as concerned with the invisible, not just the more visible practices and liturgies. Two writers whose work can help shape such a pedagogy are Charles Taylor and Lev Vygotsky.

Charles Taylor's notion of the "social imaginary" has the potential to widen our focus and offer a lens that can assist us to make sense of how children are formed in school contexts. Taylor argues that to understand culture we need to stop assuming only ideas move people. This is also a strong message in the work of James Smith.[40] Taylor suggests that beneath the surface of the cognitive and intellectual arguments of a group or institution, we have human imagination at work which helps the individual to engage with stories, myths, images, iconic hopes and dreams, and connect them with our own present and past experiences, as we imagine the world as we would like it to be.[41] Taylor suggests all groups and individuals are motivated by a "social imaginary." This helps them imagine the context of their lives and their place within its present and future. I will discuss Taylor's work more fully in chapter 8 when I address imagination and creativity.

As well, the work of Russian psychologist Lev Vygotsky discussed more broadly in chapter 5 is relevant to my discussion here. What Vygotsky's work adds is an explanation of why the relationship between teacher and learner (and I would add learner and learner) is so important. Classroom life is not just about the things we do or say to one another. Vygotsky's work emphasized the dialectical relationship between teaching and learning, and drew on the concept of *obuchenie*.[42] *Obuchenie* isn't easily translated, as it means "teaching/learning" and suggests a unified process.[43] There is no

---

40. James Smith, *Desiring the Kingdom*.

41. Taylor's work had a strong influence on James K. A. Smith's work as discussed in his excellent book, *Desiring the Kingdom: Worship, Worldview, and Cultural Formation*, which we have previously discussed.

42. I am grateful to my colleague James Pietsch for pointing me to Vygotsky's specific use of this word in his article "Classroom Culture and Relational Spaces," 15–19.

43. Weiner, *Handbook of Psychology*, 133.

equivalent English word, though some have interpreted the word as applying simply to "instruction"; however, this is far too narrow. Translators tell us that the Russian word characterizes teaching and learning as intertwined. This is an important foundational concept within the definition of pedagogy I am using in this book.

Obuchenie requires both the teacher and the student to adapt to one another. While the teacher has a position of authority and usually greater knowledge and world experience, this does not prevent both from listening to and learning from one another.[44] What Vygotsky was suggesting was a shift toward a different context for learning, one in which the relationship between teacher and student is changed. Once again, such a change requires a shift of pedagogical focus from simply transmitting knowledge or practices for students to replicate, to the creation of classrooms where students have the opportunity to see connection between the varied communities of practice they navigate each day as part of normal life. These are classrooms where teachers guide, nudge, respond, question, listen, observe, urge, teach, and reveal truth in ways students can connect to their lived experiences.

While no single metaphor seems to summarize completely the nature of the teacher's role I am advocating, one of the most helpful is that of guide. The quote from Daniel Estes at the head of this chapter reflects something of the quite complex role teachers play. In his work, Estes considers what the wisdom of Proverbs in the Bible suggests to us about the role the teacher plays. He identifies varied roles that, while not described in definitive terms, are certainly evident. Three he sees as worthy of special comment: the teacher as an expert authority, the teacher as facilitator, and the teacher as guide.[45] The teacher at times speaks and directs learning as one in possession of knowledge to be shared. As well, they act as a facilitator where students are more actively involved in the learning process. Finally, he identifies the teacher as guide where, while the teacher might still share knowledge with her students, she permits the learner great freedom to "investigate life and make decisions."[46] Estes concludes that perhaps the latter best describes the role of the teacher in Proverbs.

A number of the vignettes in this book have also demonstrated these metaphors at work in classrooms. Classrooms and schools where students

44. Vygotsky, "Thinking and Speech," 237–85.

45. Estes, *Hear, My Son*, 125–34.

46. Ibid., 130–33.

experience the teacher as facilitator and guide, not just an authority, would seem to be the situations where teachers and students listen and respond to one another best. They are places where the participants learn from each other, as interaction increases and learning becomes more dialogic and varied voices are heard.

HOW COMMUNITY PRACTICES CAN
POINT TO THE GOOD

I want to return briefly to our vignette in chapter 2—the one concerning Jackie—to discuss how practices point to the good. You will recall that Jackie was a year-eleven student from a non-Christian family with a strong group of mainly non-Christian friends who had common interests in music, film, fashion, dance, and boys. Jackie's membership in a diverse range of communities of practice required her to share in varied social and cultural practices, as well as specific priorities, values, and rules of engagement. Each community of practice in its own way promoted to her, and required from her, some sense of shared vision of the good life, that is, the things that matter and shape how we participate in word and bodily enactment. As MacIntyre reminds us, in one of the quotes that head this chapter, "every activity, every enquiry, every practice, aims at some good."[47] This is a quote we also discussed in chapter 2 when we considered my claim that education is *the whole of life of a community*, not just curriculum, teaching methods, school discipline, or even chapel services and Bible studies.

Classrooms and schools are messy places that consist of individual students who have membership in many communities of practice. Our students may or may not share a common sense of the ends towards which the life of the classroom is directed. They may also at any time have a different focus of attention and sense of the end goal of the practice at hand, not to mention their education and their imagined future.

However, as I also argued above, Aristotelian virtue ethics framed by an understanding of practice shifts attention away from the shared practices within communities and the reasons for accepting or rejecting them. While our lives have aims and goals that point us toward a specific *telos*, the key questions are which goals students will choose and how will their choices be influenced by teachers? Whether teachers are aware of their role

47. MacIntyre, *After Virtue*, 148.

in this or not, all teachers have a special role to play in influencing the *telos* of each child's life.

As I suggested in chapter 1, how schools manage the sense that the school is set within the world, but is oriented to the next, is critical to authenticity. It is in the daily response of teachers to ungodly behavior, our stance on the choice of literature and cultural texts for discussion (what's in and out), the way we relate to and deal with technology, popular culture, social media, and much more where we make clear a different *telos*. Part of this is a communication of the internal goods that are important to us, and an imagined future our students can read, understand, consider, and be attracted to. Or of course they might reject this as they try to work out their own potential place in such a future view of the good life.

My quest in this book is to offer insights that will help everyday classroom teachers understand the complexity of classroom and school life, and its difference from the life that students experience in many varied communities of practice that also make up their worlds in and outside school, communities which often have little direct relationship to what we see as school. In doing this, my hope is teachers will be able to create contexts in which they can make the goals of practices transparent, and at the same time show the tension between the intents, meanings, and differences of these practices across these varied worlds they inhabit.

The aim is for the *telos* of the varied communities we inhabit to be identified and understood as they relate to our pedagogy, classroom life, and curriculum. This will include the formal as well as the informal, whether the teacher is very much in the foreground, or is only incidental to the practices.

As researchers like Jean Lave and Etienne Wenger have demonstrated, the everyday practices of the classroom are often very different from the cultural meanings and purposes embedded within the day-to-day practices students experience in and outside school.[48] The vignette shared in chapter 2, where Chanda would not participate in school writing lessons, is an example of how the *telos* of our students' behavior and practices can be misunderstood and perceived to be distant to them. While Chanda was an active composer and writer of music outside school, she could not see that the goals of the classroom practice had any intersection with her personal goals outside the school.

As advocates of situated cognition have shown in their research, what is learned has a relationship to the specific situations or contexts in which

48. Lave and Wenger, *Situated Learning*.

these things are learned. Learning is always situated and enacted. The practices in which our students participate cannot be separated from the learning that takes place within them.[49] This is of course a point David Smith and James Smith make in arguing for their particular focus on Christian liturgical practices. My quest is for a pedagogy that is constantly attentive to where children are at in life. What issues are bothering them, and which issues should be in focus? How do I respond to the issues they face each day, and how do I connect what I try to do as a teacher as I teach a mandated curriculum with appropriate methods, with helping them learn about life?

In the communities of practice that give shape to our students' lives they "share a concern or a passion for something they do and learn how to do it better as they interact regularly."[50] The Christian teacher's greatest challenge is to focus classroom life on eternal goals and a different *telos*. In essence, to focus student lives on the kingdom of God, not earthly kingdoms. To what will we look for evidence of this different *telos*? We will see evidence of it in the practices of people, the goals and priorities of teachers, the curriculum, and the official language of the class and school. We will also see it in the stories students share, the narratives that influence and shape their lives—whether from popular culture or their world—or the shared stories that occur in the context of their lives. As we have discussed in earlier chapters, story is part of the rich stuff of the numerous communities of practice our students inhabit. Narrative is part of the way such communities enable students to not only feel included, but also to support the things that are valued as part of their shared habitus. Our students need to live the life of the classroom and school as members and participants, not observers and visitors who negotiate safe entry and exit each day to the communities that really matter to them.

There is a second key component of the life of the school and the many competing communities of practice. It is the imaginary life of our students. Taylor's discussion of the "social imaginary" above suggests that beneath the surface of many classroom interactions, the imaginations of our students are at work. This God-given imagination helps them engage with our stories, the intent of our curriculum and practices, and to reflect on their experiences of school as they try to connect them with their lives and their hoped-for goals of the future. We will consider the imagination in chapter 8, but first we will look at story in chapter 7.

49. Brown et al., "Situated Cognition and the Culture of Learning," 32–34.
50. Lave and Wenger, *Situated Learning*, 6.

7

Storytelling and Life

*I am a theologian, I have been trained too well to be able to trust claims that
I might make about what God may or may not have done to make my life
possible. I believe, however, that God made my life possible. Yet how do you
write a testimony, a witness, to testify to God's presence in your life that does
not make more of you than your life has been? How do you testify to God in a
manner that does not tempt you to say more about God than you know? These
were the conundrums I faced.*[1]

—STANLEY HAUERWAS

*The story of oneself is embedded in the history of the world, an overall narra-
tive within which all other narratives find their place.*[2]

—ALASDAIR MACINTYRE

As I have been arguing throughout this book, "education is the whole of life
of a community and the experience of its members learning to live this life
from a specific standpoint or end goal." The classroom life is a subset of the
child's complete lived experience and they share this with others in varied
ways. One of the ways this occurs is through the life stories students share
as they live and learn together.

1. Hauerwas, *Hannah's Child*, 286.
2. MacIntyre, *Three Rival Versions of Moral Enquiry*, 92.

In chapters 5 and 6, I argued one of the key tasks of the teacher is to orchestrate classroom life, accepting that our students inhabit multiple communities of practice that act to shape desires and goals for the future. Our task is not simply to plan and use curriculum practices that work to sustain programs, but to have an impact on the lives of our students. One of the ways good teachers do this is by listening to the stories of our students, for from them come insights about who they are, what they are learning, the hopes they have for their future, the things that trouble them, and the deepest desires of their hearts. Much of life is shared through story and the attentive teacher will listen carefully to them and facilitate their sharing. This is listening and perhaps reading with intent for the echoes of life ambitions, challenges, hopes, and fears. In this chapter I want to consider how story is at work in classrooms and how important it is for the formation of our students' hoped-for futures.

THE RELATIONSHIP OF STORY TO "LOVE," "DESIRE," AND "COMMUNITY"

When I use the word *story*, I am using it in a very broad sense. I am not speaking simply of "a fictional narrative shorter than a novel."[3] Rather, I am using it as a variant of "narrative," that is, "a spoken or written account of connected events."[4] This broader definition includes the real and imaginary, true and fictional, story, recount, even anecdote. While narrative is the broader term, I deliberately use story, for it carries with it the implication of something with an imagined, constructed, purposeful, and communicative nature. It includes factual recounts and passionately held views expressed in narrative form by way of illustration, anecdote, poem, song, and so on. Stories are deeply personal things, and have purposes that go well beyond entertainment or information. Our stories reflect our history, values, beliefs, priorities, and intent when we share them. Of course, having a right perspective on our own story is challenging. As the quote from Stanley Hauerwas at the head of this chapter indicates it is difficult to write or share one's testimony about God's work in our lives, without making more of our ourselves than we should. Making sense of my own

3. Merriam-Webster online dictionary, https://www.merriam-webster.com/dictionary/story.

4. Merriam-Webster online dictionary, https://www.merriam-webster.com/dictionary/narrative.

life has been a challenge. I will do my best to share this later in the chapter, and God willing, I won't do it "in a manner that does not tempt [me] to say more about God than [I] know."[5]

To be human is to understand our God-given desire to know our purpose in life and to seek fulfillment in the "hoped for," the ultimate quest of each life. In life, we are immersed within an intertextual cacophony of stories that shape and influence the things we desire. From these stories, we read various representations of the future, and alternative visions of what Aristotle first called "human flourishing."[6] In a sense, we are taught, perhaps even lured, by these pictures, these visions of the future.

Stories are also more than disconnected and isolated accounts; they typically have a relationship to other larger metanarratives. Christian Smith suggests that narratives "seek to convey the significance and meaning of events by situating their interaction with or influence on other events and actions in a single, interrelated account."[7] They include a set of characters or players, both subjects and objects of the action. They have a plot that gives shape to the action with a beginning, middle, and end, and they seek to communicate significant points or messages. Smith suggests that in this age, dominated by the power of reason and evidence, and the rational over the creative, we are nonetheless still creatures who are "the makers, tellers, and believers of narrative construals of existence, history, and purpose."[8] We make stories and in turn we are made by them.

This making of us is shaped at least in part by the stories we absorb, give expression to, and help create. James K. A. Smith suggests this is no simple cognitive process.[9] Rather, we are embodied creatures who absorb the stories of life and engage in rituals and cultural practices that shape our desires and our vision of the good life. This argument draws on Charles Taylor's concept of the "social imaginary" mentioned briefly in chapter 6. Taylor argues that societies are given direction by an imagined and hoped-for view of the world. This is not expressed simply in "theoretical terms, but is carried in images, stories and legends."[10] Humans are not given their major focus and direction simply by reasoning, but also by the imagination.

5. Hauerwas, *Hannah's Child*, 286.

6. Cairney, "Storytelling and Life," 5.

7. Christian Smith, *Moral, Believing Animals*, 65–66.

8. Ibid., 64.

9. James Smith, *Desiring the Kingdom*, 41.

10. Taylor, *Modern Social Imaginaries*, 25.

Taylor's use of the term "social imaginary" is quite deliberate. Much broader than an intellectual understanding of reality, his focus is on how people "imagine their social surroundings."[11] While his category is a little slippery, and doesn't address all we know about memory, thinking, and knowledge,[12] the point is worth making. Our imaginations are primed by the narratives we experience in daily life, and thus primed, we develop desires and views of the good life, accept shared group understandings, and make sense of our experiences. The use of the term social imaginary emphasizes the rich social context in which we make sense of the world, a context influenced as much or more by story as by deliberate reasoning. This is not to suggest our stories are not subjected at times to analysis and critique, but they are often born in life moments where our imaginations are captured, even if only momentarily, by narrative, whether heard, read, seen, or experienced.

The stories that are part of our experience thus shape our vision of the good life, give focus to our desires, and direction to our lives. In exploring the relationship between love and community, Oliver O'Donovan reminds us of Augustine's statement that a community is "a gathered multitude of rational beings united by agreeing to share the things they love."[13] Hauerwas, also when exploring aspects of community, suggests that in essence, a group of people come to see a common "view of the good," and are hence capable of common action, cultural practices, and identity.[14]

James Smith agrees with Taylor that our hopes, goals, desires, and views are influenced by our imaginative experience of the world, including its stories. Echoing Augustine, Smith argues we inhabit the world not primarily as thinkers or believers, but as "more affective, embodied creatures who make our way in the world more by feeling our way around it."[15] Once

---

11. Ibid., 23.

12. My research on text comprehension and later research on intertextuality suggests that thinking is never detached from the social and textual context within which we learn, remember, set goals, and so on. Taylor's examples concerning the common understandings necessary to carry out collective practices parallels work in cognitive psychology and discourse theory. In these fields, for example, they are referred to as "scripts" or "schemata." See Rumelhart, "Schemata," which discusses the theoretical work, and Cairney, *Teaching Reading Comprehension*, which discusses the application of this work.

13. O'Donovan, *Common Objects of Love*, 20–24.

14. Stanley Hauerwas also talks about this process of community formation as being "story-formed." Hauerwas, "A Story-Formed Community," 171–99.

15. James Smith, *Desiring the Kingdom*, 47.

again, quoting Augustine,[16] he suggests we are above all things "agents of love, which takes the structure of desire or longing."[17]

Smith argues our desires are aimed at specific ends or goals, and set the trajectory for our lives:

> A vision of the good life captures our hearts and imaginations . . . by painting a picture of what it looks like for us to flourish and live well. This is why such pictures are communicated most powerfully in stories, legends, myths, plays, novels, and films rather than dissertations, messages and monographs.[18]

To be human is to understand our God-given desire to understand our purpose and to seek fulfillment in the "hoped for," the ultimate quest of each life. Our quests, in a sense, are story shaped, for they are filled with stories that influence the things we desire.[19] And from these stories, we read various representations of the future, and alternative visions of human flourishing. In a sense, we are taught, or as James Smith suggests, perhaps even lured, by these "pictures," these visions of the future. But of course, stories move and challenge us through their depiction of tragedy, not just hope, at times in juxtaposition. Bruce Smith suggests that the "feeling that the universe as a whole to which we belong is indifferent to justice and to fairness is part of the constituent experience of tragedy."[20]

This connection between hope and tragedy is a key theme of literature and life. When confronted with tragedy in story (in whatever form), we are faced with contradictions. In a sense, Smith argues, the tragedy of literature "prepares us for our own death."[21] And of course in the Bible we see literature taking seriously all of the contradictions that tragedies raise. For within the Bible, we are challenged to imagine the reality that we live in "an outside-Eden world . . . where we live out the consequences of our estrangement from God for our disobedience before God."[22] But of course in the Bible's story it declares that God "has come amongst us into this

---

16. Augustine, *Augustine*, 290.

17. James Smith, *Desiring the Kingdom*, 50.

18. Ibid., 53.

19. Cairney, "Storytelling and Life," 5.

20. Bruce Smith, "Hope and Tragedy, in Life and Literature," 9–10.

21. Ibid., 10.

22. Ibid., 12.

outside-Eden world with its contradictions and pending menaces; he has come amongst us in the person of his son, and he has done so as man."[23]

Story has the power to challenge, move us emotionally, cause us to reflect on life in all its dimensions, and to seek after hope as we deal with all of life's emotions including love, hate, fear, confidence, chaos, certainty, weakness, strength, success, and failure. Given that story is an important influence on what we come to love and desire, it follows that it is potentially formative for our attitude toward the ultimate object of love—the God of the universe—who has made us for a future kingdom and an everlasting hope and glory. The significance of story for teaching should be obvious. It operates at multiple levels in the life of the school. At one level, students learn about the world through story. But at a deeper level they begin to imagine their own futures, their deepest desires, and the good life which they seek. As well, story is experienced in many forms: written, spoken, sung, viewed, heard, and experienced. In our world, we can be confronted and moved by books, advertising, movies, and music. This of course occurs in the everydayness of life, whether at school, work, home, or in the world at large. I want to share my personal story to illustrate what I mean.

MY PERSONAL STORY

I have no recollection of ever being read to as a child. There were few books in my home and my early years were not characterized by a mother or father curled up with me, reading great literature. But in middle age I was to reflect on my early literary experiences and conclude that I had lived in a home rich in anecdote, song, and narratives, and that these had helped shape me. While my parents seemed to do little to encourage a love of literature or writing, my world was filled with my parents' stories, and in particular the texts and stories that had spoken to them.

My father was a consummate oral storyteller, and my mother an entertainer and singer who filled my life with opera, ballads, and popular music. There is no doubt my father's stories of events that had shaped him also served to shape me. He shared his life story through anecdotes and narratives, which reflected overarching metanarratives related to his view of the "good life."[24] Some of his stories were no doubt true, others half true, and some perhaps mere constructions. Many were influenced by his brand

23. Ibid., 12.
24. Christian Smith, *Moral, Believing Animals*, 63–94.

of Marxism, its critique of the nature of capitalism, and its views on the exploitation of the workers by the bourgeois. He drew on his experiences and those of his family in post-Victorian Glasgow, his life in decaying tenement housing, his work and advocacy in the coal mines of Australia as a leader in the most militant industrial union in the nation, and his experience of the Depression and World War II. And when he was drunk, he would share many of life's deeper stories of tragedy and disappointment.

My father's immigration from Scotland was a critical event in the family's life. His father left for Australia alone to seek a better life just after WWI, and my grandmother was left to raise eleven children alone. It was to be two years before the rest of the family arrived in Newcastle to join my grandfather. However, my father's view of what was important in life appeared to be shaped by more than just family experiences. His stories often reflected the importance he placed on a desire for financial security, a home of his own, freedom of expression, and an egalitarian life in the promised land of Australia. The loathsome plots of mine owners, the decaying housing of an incompetent government, the might of workers united. All of these hopes, hates, and desires were no doubt drawn, at least in part, from the things he'd read and the stories of others and life.

As a child, my father's stories washed over me and engaged me. So too did the stories of my maternal grandfather, with whom I stayed during most school holidays—a godly, creative, and intelligent man. He was a brilliant inventor and businessman who constantly quoted the Scriptures (especially the Psalms and Proverbs), and he recited Australian and Scottish poetry and ballads whenever we did things together. I saw no place for God in my life until I was thirty-one, but I can see with hindsight that my own emerging view of the good life was based in part on my rejection of many of my father's ideas. But they were also connected to an embracing of the alternative narratives of my grandparents, and later as an adult, a growing group of Christian friends and chance contacts, who had different hopes and desires than mine.[25] This is the way narrative works in our lives. It touches us, teaches us, and in time shapes us.

The stories of my father, grandfather, mother, and significant others, in one sense, were a product of their lives. By telling their stories they revealed some sense of their perceived good life, and the quest within each of us to find it. These stories also captured my imagination and influenced

25. O'Donovan, *Common Objects of Love*, 20–24.

my own vision for the future, or as Charles Taylor describes it, my "social imaginary."[26]

THE ROLE OF STORY IN CHRISTIAN FORMATION

There are many possible discussions surrounding the place of story in Christian formation, but I want to discuss three different complementary explanations for the key place of story in children's lives and the role they play in schooling.

Story is helpful in Enabling Children to Consider the Path Between This Life and the Next

As I have already argued in this book, Christian formation in the school and family is about nurturing and growing the citizen on this earth with an orientation toward the next. All we hope children to become in the world now should be directed to what they are destined to become in the kingdom of God. The focus of a Christian *paideia*[27]—the formation of the child—is not the building of better citizens to successfully take their place in civil society,[28] but rather the maturing of children in Christ. As Paul tells the Philippian church, "our citizenship is in heaven, and from it we await a Savior, the Lord Jesus Christ, who will transform our lowly body to be like his glorious body, by the power that enables him even to subject all things to himself (Phil 3:20–21)."

Parents and Christian teachers will of course go first to the Bible as the foundation of their quest to influence the maturing of children in Christ. But story, more generally, has an essential place in negotiating a path between the cultural experiences of citizens of earth and a longing for the citizenship of heaven to be fully realized. This is critical in developing a

---

26. Taylor, *Modern Social Imaginaries*, 106.

27. In another publication I discuss the biblical roots of the word *paideia*, which for first-century Greeks meant a process of becoming fully human, or of young men becoming citizens—to make the point that pedagogy is central to biblical education whether within the family, church, or school. Cairney et al., *New Perspectives in Anglican Education*.

28. Of course, this is not to reject the importance of citizenship on earth and the importance this plays in education, but it must be seen as subordinate to a right focus on the kingdom of God.

distinctive pedagogy. Children experience stories in their lives which can shape their emerging and imagined view of the good life and their hoped-for future. These stories are experienced in books, from television, video games, and from the mouths of others. So prolific are stories in the life of the child that we need to ask how Christian parents and teachers are to intervene in the vast array of stories that fill the child's world.

One response is to embark on an almost futile interrogative and critical stance, monitoring and listening to the stories children hear, and identifying points of departure from Christian belief, or alternatively, teaching only from the Bible and trying to shield children from the world's stories. But this limited critical reading of the world and its texts, will do little more than create Christian enclaves within the home, school, and family set against the world. Kevin Vanhoozer argues, to the contrary, that the task of parents and teachers is to help students read culture, and so it is unwise simply to sift, sort, and reject it.[29] We must understand culture before we can exclude or embrace it. Christian pedagogy must not reflect either of the extreme responses to the world—that is, uncritical acceptance, or rejection in response to the sinful rebellion of the world. Chris Swann discusses this point in detail in a recent essay, rejecting these extremes on the basis that Christians and non-Christians alike inhabit God's good but distorted creation.[30] Simple black-and-white responses are not adequate; robust interaction with culture requires effort and wisdom. We must help our students evaluate the stories which are part of the culture in which they are immersed.

The role of the Christian parent or teacher in helping children to negotiate their way through a world of story requires a degree of courage, risk-taking and, most significantly, trust that they are ultimately in God's hands, not just our own. It is very tempting for parents and teachers to exclude stories and texts from a child's world simply because they are written by non-Christians, or contain ideas which do not conform to our own metanarratives of the world. This is particularly the case if these clash with our biblical understanding. But our children need to navigate their way through the mire of alternative views of the good life. What's more, within the secular texts of their world they will encounter not only echoes[31] of the wisdom of God, but knowledge that is helpful for their formation.

29. Vanhoozer, "What is Everyday Theology?"

30. Swann, "Humanising the Monster," 16.

31. As J. R. R. Tolkien argued and demonstrated in his writing of fantasy, in our

The competing metanarratives of life are not mutually exclusive, nor is truth only in the hands of the Christian author or the day-to-day stories and reflections of the Christian teacher. This idea has also been explored in a paper by William Tate.[32] Tate discusses the intriguing notion of "secular parables" in the work of Karl Barth, who in turn developed it from the thoughts of John Calvin.[33] Tate describes Barth's secular parables as "true words" that can be "actual words" as well as "other kinds of cultural artefacts—spoken (whether literally or metaphorically) from outside the walls of the Church."[34] For if, as we discussed in chapter 6, God is the source of all truth, then God can speak truth through secular writing as well. If we accept that God can use secular writers to communicate truth, then we need to very carefully approach the way we privilege, or censor, some of the literature within our schools. What is clear is we need to prepare our children to navigate the tricky waters of the stories they will encounter in life.

Story is an Example of the Outworking of God-Given Creativity and Imagination

When I became a Christian, it was in response to a sermon preached on Matthew 11:28–30:

> Come to me, all you who are weary and burdened, and I will give you rest. Take my yoke upon you and learn from me, for I am gentle and humble in heart, and you will find rest for your souls. For my yoke is easy and my burden is light.

I heard these verses for the first time on my second visit to a church, other than for a few weddings and one or two funerals. These words pierced my heart. I was convicted of my own sinfulness, I had a great sense of shame, and a sudden desire to know who Jesus was. I went home, hid in the bathroom and my response was simply to call out to God. I pleaded with him to make himself known, and to help me understand and believe.

---

stories and our attempts to describe our experiences, our hopes and our aspirations, there is a sense in which they must all be read against this central biblical narrative, "the greatest story of them all."

32. Tate, "Karl Barth's Secular Parables," 22–26.

33. For a good discussion of Calvin's notion of the *sensus divinitatis*, or sense of the divine in human nature, and its implications for education, see Jensen, "The Creature Who Learns," 41–45.

34. Tate, "Karl Barth's Secular Parables," 22.

I stood there in tears, not due to having reached the end of ten years of rea-soning and attempts to comprehend the Scriptures, but as someone deeply convicted of my sinfulness before God. I had caught a glimpse of God's kingdom and his Son. God had brought me to a point where I was able to imagine Jesus, not merely as man, but as the risen Son of God. I was able to see that in a world marked by ugliness as well as beauty, there was a deeper meaning and purpose.

The gospel of Christ met me at a point where my vision of the future and the good life could not be satisfied by what I had been pursuing in life. God was able to use my imagination, as well as my powers of reasoning and comprehension, to move me from rebellion to new life. My deepest burdens, and my weariness from trying to solve my doubts and frustra-tions in life, could be taken from me. But this required me to yoke myself to Jesus, rather than selfish ambition, the quest for comfort and material security, and my proud reliance on intellect and worldly success. I was able to imagine how God had sent his Son as man and God to die a death I did not witness, in a place and a time beyond my experience, for a person I sud-denly knew for the first time. I discuss this example in a slightly different way in chapter 8, when we consider imagination.

N. T. Wright argues we need "imagination to cope with"[35] making sense of a world that is both beautiful and ugly. I needed to make an imagi-native leap from my view of the world, shaped by the story of my life, and the various influences on it. I needed to see that the world could only have a future—and indeed I could only have a future—because of a Jewish man crucified two thousand years ago: Jesus.

God gave us imagination as part of our human nature. We were made in his image as creatures who can imagine. Imagination isn't something to be repressed or controlled by reason or logic, but is part of who we are, and is to be enjoyed, celebrated, and cultivated. I will discuss this point in full in the next chapter. Story is part of the way we recall the past, make sense of our world and, imagine the future God has planned for us. What's more, the reading of Scripture and our ability to make sense of it requires our ability to imagine that which the words signify. As I read the Scriptures, I am constantly moved by the words and what I am able to imagine and grasp through them. I cannot read the Psalms without constantly calling upon my imagination. How else could I make sense of the imagery of the psalmist's words, "I long to dwell in your tent forever and take refuge in

35. Wright, "Bible and Christian Imagination," 5.

the shelter of your wings" (Ps 61:4). Or, how can I read Revelation 21 and not gain some sense of the magnitude and glory of the New Jerusalem? My imagination helps me to read the words of Scripture, and grasp something of the wonder they signify and communicate to me.

It is important to stress I am not suggesting imagination has a primary role in God's illumination of his truth and purposes. As J. R. R. Tolkien suggested, art and the imagination simply assist us in the understanding of our world.[36] Art, music, and literature give us a fuller insight into God's world and his plans for it. Trevor Hart argued powerfully in the 2008 New College Lectures that, "artistic vision is no matter of gainsaying or superseding our world, but precisely of glimpsing the richness and the possibilities latent within the creative vision of God himself."[37]

Our God made us to inhabit a world rich in potential. In his wisdom, kindness, and grace he bestowed on us the potential to imagine and act creatively as we explore and make sense of a world which Psalm 33 tells us was created by God's word! "For he spoke, and it came to be; he commanded, and it stood firm" (Ps 33:9).

Literature and Stories as Pointers to God's Ultimate Story

As my personal story indicates, narrative and storytelling are inescapable for all of us, as it is an essential part of our humanity. English linguist Harold Rosen suggested much of human existence is dependent on story, and that it helps us move through the seeming chaos of life to understanding. As well, insights into life itself are shared through story. Much human wisdom, knowledge, and understanding has been passed down through the ages as story. While objects and images have a place in the recording and communicating of people's histories, words and the genre of story seem to have long held a special place in human existence.

Alasdair MacIntyre, in *After Virtue*, suggests that "man [sic] is in his actions and practices, as well as in his fictions, essentially a story-telling animal."[38] We frequently think in narrative, and pass on our personal history, envision the future and speak of the present predominantly through story. As his quote suggests at the head of the chapter, our personal life story has a relationship to all other stories. They are,

36. Tolkien, *Tree and Leaf*, 56.

37. Hart, *Givenness, Grace and Gratitude*.

38. MacIntyre, *After Virtue*, 195.

embedded in the history of the world, an overall narrative within which all other narratives find their place.[39]

MacIntyre's point echoes in some ways that which J. R. R. Tolkien uttered to C. S. Lewis about the central narrative of life. Before sharing this point, we need to recall that the central theme of the Bible, in effect God's view of his world, has been termed "salvation history," for its narrative traces God's relationship with his creation, particularly mankind.[40] The Bible's story offers us a view of humanity and our relation to the one who created us. In the beginning, God created the heavens and the earth (Gen 1:1). He spoke into existence the light and the darkness, the waters and the land, vegetation, the sun, the moon and the stars, living creatures of all kinds. Finally, he made man and from him woman, and it was good. But the rebellion of man and woman led to the wrath of God, and a change in their relationship to him. And yet, in love and mercy, God had a plan of redemption for the rebellious creatures he had made. He, the mighty and holy God of the universe, would restore this broken relationship through the sacrificial gift of his own Son as an atonement for sins. And one day, there would be the consummation, when Christ would return to create a new heaven and new earth, and his followers would live with him for eternity, worshipping our God.

J. R. R. Tolkien, in a famous conversation with C. S. Lewis while walking through the campus at Oxford one frosty night, suggested to Lewis that "just as a word is an invention about an object or an idea, so a story can be an invention about Truth." And he continued, "The Christian story is the greatest story of them all. Because it's the real story. The historical event that fulfils the tales and shows us what they mean."[41]

But surely, you might say, I can't claim God's story of redemption is evident in all literature? In a sense, I am claiming this. While it might be difficult to see much of the light of God in some of the trashy novels you might pick up in the local book store, it may ultimately contain truth, and all truth derives from God.[42] Barth saw it this way, drawing on Calvin's idea that all of creation is the "theatre of God's glory," and that literature, even

---

39. MacIntyre, *Three Rival Versions of Moral Enquiry*, 92.

40. Speed, "What Might have Been," 12–13.

41. Ware, *God and the Fairy Tale*, 2.

42. Tate, "Karl Barth's Secular Parables," 22–26.

written by the pagan, can be used by God as part of his general revelation to mankind. One's personal story also has a relationship to this grand narrative.

Tate, when speaking of the relationship of secular writing to this central narrative, cites Barth's use of parable as relevant. All stories can point to a meaning beyond the basic narrative. Even secular parables might be used by God to speak to particular people in specific contexts. I, too, believe that just as God uses the preaching of biblical literature to reveal inexplicable meanings at times for the preacher's audience, so too, secular parables can be used by God to point to the central narrative of God's redemptive plans for his creation.[43]

Understanding that God can reveal himself through all of creation, including the works of humankind, should free us to embrace personal testimonies, secular literature, indigenous dreamtime stories from varied nations, folk tales, and even the anecdotes of life as vehicles for God's revelation of truth to us. This is not to suggest that all that is written in the name of literature should be freely shared with our children, but it does allow us to avoid the extremes of disengagement with the literature and stories of the world or total assimilation and acceptance.[44]

I wrote a number of years ago in my book *Pathways to Literacy*[45] that literature is not just about the enjoyment of story. I claimed it is about life and one's world. As such, literature and stories do much more than entertain; they can act as

a. mirrors to enable readers to reflect on life problems and circumstances;
b. sources of knowledge;
c. sources of ideological challenge;
d. a means to peer into the past, and the future;
e. vehicles to other places;
f. a way to reflect on inner struggles;
g. an introduction to the realities of life and death; and
h. a way to raise and discuss varied social issues.

What I am suggesting is literature as a form of narrative offers readers endless possibilities for exploration, imagination, learning, and challenge

43. Ibid., 24–25.
44. Swann, "Humanising the Monster," 16.
45. Cairney, *Pathways to Literacy*, 77–78.

and that it serves a key role in school education, particularly in the elementary school years.[46] This role of literature is much broader and less explicitly connected to biblical truth than traditional Bible stories for children. But nonetheless, stories can point to, and illustrate, God's salvation narrative and his work in our lives. Stories can be used by God as part of his general revelation and common grace to us, both to enrich our imagined and hoped-for view of the good life, and in the process draw attention to aspects of the human condition. As a result of this, stories can bring into focus truth, beauty, and goodness, as well as human virtues that reflect the grace and providence of God. This point will be made in a much more detailed way in chapter 8 when we consider imagination.

You don't have to try very hard to see how literature often echoes (even if imperfectly) God's foundational story of salvation. In E. B. White's classic tale, *Charlotte's Web*,[47] the rescue of a pig by a spider at one level might seem trivial, but it is a story of salvation nonetheless, and in its own way is a faint echo of the ultimate act of sacrifice by God in redeeming his children through his Son.

While Christians often seek books for their children that explicitly present the gospel, literature can work in many ways. Obviously, we will continue to see biblical narrative as the key way to teach God's truth to our children. But we mustn't underestimate the role of literature and story as part of God's general revelation to us. There will be special value in literature that more explicitly points to the central salvation narrative. Books like the *Chronicles of Narnia* series by C. S. Lewis and *Dangerous Journey* by John Bunyan[48]—both of which explicitly allegorize the gospel—have unique value in communicating biblical truth. But there is much literature that would be seen as secular literature that nevertheless deals with biblical themes and categories, and which has much to say about the human condition that is consistent with Scripture.[49]

The challenge for teachers and parents is in this third category of literature, but this is where the gospel and popular culture can meet. These are the texts of television, film, children's and adolescent literature

---

46. Cairney, *Other Worlds*.

47. White, *Charlotte's Web*.

48. Bunyan, *Dangerous Journey*. This is an abridged version of the well-known allegory *The Pilgrim's Progress*.

49. I've written a number of posts about literature on a blog I write titled *Literacy, Families & Learning*. It can be found at http://trevorcairney.blogspot.com.au/.

(including most set school texts), and the world in general. Children need to negotiate these, learn to read them, and understand the themes, ideology, values, worldview, and images of humanity they contain. We should offer such books as raw material for a form of Christian critical literacy. This type of literature is a vital part of school education, and is in a sense at the very boundaries of the territory where matters of faith and belief are explored. Parents and teachers need to be a vital part of this. Not as censors and thought police, but as participants in literary dialogue and discussion pointing always to biblical truth.

HOW DO WE APPROACH THE ROLE OF STORIES IN CHILDREN'S LIVES?

So, what are we to do with stories as teachers and even parents? First, I believe we need to understand the significant role they play in children's formation. This has been the major task of this chapter. We need to understand the power and impact stories will have on children's reading of the past and hoped-for future. Second, we need to engage as storytellers and interpreters of stories in children's lives, nurturing their growing faith, answering their unending questions in the light of God's word, and encouraging their emerging assumptions, views and hopes for the good life. Finally, we need to continue to consider how story, as a vehicle for the expansion of children's imaginations, can open their eyes to the God of the universe. This of course will be the focus of the next chapter where imagination and creativity will be considered as a part of our humanity, and God's work in drawing us to himself.

The role of story and imagination in children's formation begins in the first weeks of life as they experience the rhymes, songs, sounds, and words we share with them. It continues as they are immersed in the stories of daily life and an emerging array of multimodal textual experiences. It is strengthened or weakened as the child begins to read these stories in the light of the Bible's rich salvation history and wisdom. It is challenged in late childhood as the stories of popular culture clash with those that once seemed unquestionable and unassailable. Finally, it is tested in the cut and thrust of teenage and adult life, as all previous assumptions are contested by alternative understandings of what it means to be human, what our purpose is, and why we are here.

How we position ourselves within, alongside, and as part of the stories our students experience and tell is critical. As I have argued above, in one sense, almost any story heard, read, viewed, or experienced can be used for their good, if read and understood in the light of God's eternal story of forgiveness, redemption, grace, and hope in Christ. This learning takes time and requires the close involvement of teachers and parents in children's lives: listening to them, answering their questions, and seeking to understand what they are grappling with day by day. We need to hear their stories, tell them our own, and share the stories of others, always on the foundation of a growing knowledge of God's promises revealed in Christ by his word.

8

Imagination and Life

At a precognitive level, we are attracted to a vision of the good life that has been painted for us in stories and myths, images and icons. It is not primarily our minds that are captivated but rather our imaginations that are captured, and when our imagination is hooked, we're hooked.[1]

—JAMES K. A. SMITH

This chapter considers the important topic of the human imagination. It has a close relationship to chapter 7 concerning story. Imagination is a key part of our life and humanity God uses to draw us to himself. As well, it is important for learning, community formation, discovery, and creativity. Without imagination, we would be a pale shadow of what God meant us to be.

A foundational assumption of this chapter, and indeed the book, is God took on flesh in the person of Jesus, and in doing so left humanity to live with a tension and interaction between the material and the immaterial. Hart suggests imagination, language, and literature have a vital part to play in "brokering this hypostatic union of matter and meaning within the human creature."[2] The use of the human imagination spreads more broadly than language and literature to include physical and creative actions, strategic thinking, innovation, and so on. The varied human outputs of life are at least partly expressed through our imaginations and longings, as we seek God and experience all he intended for us.[3]

1. James Smith, *Desiring the Kingdom*, 54.
2. Hart, *Between the Image and the Word*, 1.
3. I owe Trevor Hart a great debt in helping me to clarify the direction of my work.

As a consequence, rather than being suspicious of human imagination leading us into fanciful worlds, we need to recognize that God, who is himself imaginative, made us as creatures who can use our imaginations to understand his purposes for us. God's revelation is connected closely to our capacities to imagine. Imagination acts to perpetuate a fragment of beauty already in the world.[4] Our creative responses are part of the way we receive and reciprocate the knowledge and beauty of God.

WHAT IS THE IMAGINATION?

In one of the most important recent books on the imagination, Gene Veith and Matthew Ristuccia suggest imagination is "the power of the mind to form a mental image, that is, to think in pictures or other sensory representations."[5] The imagination is expressed and used in varied ways, including our words, emotions, actions, and imaginings. What's more, these very activities of the mind can reveal knowledge and truth, as well as directing our passions and motivations. But in some ways the definition of Veith and Ristuccia does not go quite far enough. I see imagination as even broader. I see it as the intellectual activity of the mind that connects prior and new knowledge and experiences with our grasping after the unknown. It is part of the way we make sense of and respond to our world, but it also ponders the world beyond. The application of the type of imagination I am discussing is neither simply constructive, analytical, or logical thinking, nor is it whimsical, ungrounded thinking, disconnected from data, evidence, and the senses. Bernard Meland suggested that beyond "constructive understanding" is another level of application of the imagination, that is implicated in questions or reflections on one's human destiny. This he suggested requires metaphysics and theology as well. Only at the intersection of these varied resources for thinking and imagining can we grapple with truth and the unknown.[6]

His various publications and the lectures he delivered at New College in 2008 and 2015 were insightful and challenging. Having the opportunity as host to interact with Trevor was very helpful. Our conversations were rich and stimulating. These opportunities have played a key role in the development of my thinking in this area, as have the publications of his colleagues at the Institute for Theology, Imagination and the Arts (ITIA) at the University of St. Andrews Scotland.

4. Hart, *Between the Image and the Word*, 2–6.

5. Veith and Ristuccia, *Imagination Redeemed*, 13.

6. Meland, *Higher Education and the Human Spirit*, 22–29.

Drawing on the work of Richard Kearney,[7] Trevor Hart suggests imagination is "pervasive [and] a feature of our existence, [and is close] to the heart of our existence."[8] He argues it is a critical feature of our humanity, with many connections to the mundane and everyday activities of life. It can involve mental activities like "expecting, planning, exploring, fearing, hoping, believing, remembering, recognizing, analyzing, empathizing, loving, conjecturing, fantasizing, pretending," as well as the more specialized creative activities of life that also reflect our ability to imagine. These include of course, language, art, literature, music, and invention.[9]

Veith and Ristuccia remind us human imagination also allows us to "relive the past and anticipate the future."[10] Our God "made us as imaginative beings and placed us in a world which calls forth from us responses of an imaginative sort if we are to indwell it meaningfully and well . . . Life in all its fullness is from top to bottom, from beginning to end, a highly imaginative affair."[11]

One thing to stress at the outset is imagination isn't simply a fanciful invention of mind. Imagination is always related to knowledge in one form or another. Reason is never very far away from our imaginings. Our knowledge and reason are related to our imagination. The imagination is implicated as we seek to understand our world, the things we find hard to grasp, and those ideas that seem beyond our present understanding. Scientists, craftsmen and women, writers, builders, and doctors imagine futures in which they build on knowledge and know-how, to make, create, mend, and have an impact on the world.

Anthony Esolen suggests imagination, memory, and knowledge are not incompatible but related:

> A developed memory is a wondrous and terrible storehouse of things seen and heard and done. It can do what no mere search engine on the Internet can do. It can call up apparently unrelated things at once, molding them into a whole impression, or a new thought.[12]

---

7. Kearney, *Poetics of Imagining*, 1.

8. Hart, *Between the Image and the Word*, 5.

9. Ibid., 5.

10. Veith and Ristuccia, *Imagination Redeemed*, 13–15.

11. Hart, *Between the Image and the Word*, 5.

12. Esolen, *Ten Ways to Destroy the Imagination of Your Child*, 9.

Whether we read, listen, view, smell, touch hear, or even experience our world emotionally, imagination is intellectual activity of the mind that connects prior and new knowledge and experiences. It is part of the way we make sense of our world and respond. Imagination involves more than art, music, drama, dance, writing, and reading, all of which of course require it and stimulate it. We imagine also to consider possible futures, memories of our past, and our quest to make sense of all sensory inputs, and engage in our world. The imagination is also part of the way God reaches out to us, convicts us, inspires us, and reveals the truth of his word as well as his plans for us. It is a key part of the way he draws us to himself.

IMAGINATION AND THE LIFE OF FAITH

Imagination is not simply a gift to some—it is available to all. Martin Buber suggested at an education conference in 1925 that imagination and creativity are not developed over time. Rather, all people are born as creative beings. God places within us what he called an "originator instinct," and creativity grows out of this imaginative God-given disposition. While we might stifle and restrict imagination in the child, it is not something parents and teachers develop in them, for it exists in us from the beginning and is part of our humanity.[13]

Imagination is also evident in and required to read God's word. Walter Brueggemann considered the role of poetry in the Old Testament. He challenges us to engage and consider the key role imagination plays in the poetry of the Psalms, Proverbs, and the prophets. He suggests the idiom "breaks and shatters the dominant universe of discourse." The poetic imagination can also facilitate and support prophecy. The biblical poet writing impressionistically can draw readers into irony, metaphor, and parables, enabling the reader to maintain some critical distance while seeking meaning.[14] Hence, poetry can reveal meanings that would be beyond our grasp if not arranged just this way.

Prophetic poetry takes the reader "inside the life experiences which might be treated externally as only ethical or political."[15] Prophets are not simply poets just interested in language and the emotion of life, they

13. Buber, *Between Man and Man*, 99–100.
14. Brueggemann, *The Creative Word*, 52.
15. Ibid., 53.

grapple with other worlds and possibilities. There is a "tension of continuity between the present world and the promised world."[16]

Veith and Ristuccia also stress the broad presence and application of the imagination and suggest "we cannot help but use our imaginations."[17] Using a series of biblical excursions into the Old Testament book of Ezekiel, and discussion from literature, the arts, philosophy and psychology, they offer biblical insights into how God uses our imagination to reach us. They argue that, using his imagination, Ezekiel is able to understand as he experiences the visions, but of course reason was always working in parallel as Ezekiel tried to make sense of the visions God was giving him.[18]

A. W. Tozer, in his book *The Pursuit of God*[19], discusses the difference between a scribe and a prophet. He suggests the church needs to hear the "tender voice of the saint who has penetrated the veil and has gazed with inward eye upon the wonder that is God," rather than simply being told by someone what they had read (the "scribe"). Matthew Ristuccia makes the point that Ezekiel exemplifies the prophet in Tozer's text, someone who is able to see what the scribe cannot, because unlike the scribe, his imagination has been captured as God reveals truth through the visions.[20] So, while we know God reveals truth through his word by the power of his Spirit, our imaginations are an important way in which this truth is made known to us. Veith and Ristuccia suggest with the aid of the imagination "meaning is made . . . a vision for life is set . . . mind and heart and will converge."[21]

How else are we able to forgive our enemy, for logically our instinct is to stay away from enemies, think badly of them, perhaps even oppose them, and seek to do them harm. But of course, the love of God, the work of the Holy Spirit, and our forgiveness in Christ, is meant to lead us to respond in love! God can use our imaginations to help us see our enemies in a different light. Once again, how else can I understand and grasp Jesus' hard teaching in the beatitudes in Matthew's Gospel, that I am to not just tolerate my enemies, but to love them?

16. Ibid., 53.

17. Veith and Ristuccia, *Imagination Redeemed*, 15.

18. Ibid., 49.

19. Tozer, *The Pursuit of God*, 56–67.

20. Veith and Ristuccia, *Imagination Redeemed*, 14.

21. Ibid., 29.

> You have heard that it was said, "Love your neighbor and hate your enemy." But I tell you, love your enemies and pray for those who persecute you. (Matt 5:43–44)

Christian conversions are characterized by stories of how God uses our imaginations to ignite faith and to draw people to himself. Hebrews 11 and 12 offer us a gallery of greats in the faith. And yet, as we read through this motley group of people, who at times failed more than they succeeded in showing faith, we see people who like us were seized by God and were able to imagine a future that counteracted what minds might have been telling them was logical. Faith and imagination are never far away from one another.

God uses our imaginations as he draws us toward himself. When I hear stories of acts of Christian conversion, I am always stunned at how God can use a verse or two of Scripture to draw us toward himself. And yet, the testimony of the one drawn toward him can seem so different from another reading of the same verse. God's use of Matthew 11:28–30 to convict me of my sin and to bring me to my knees is in stark contrast to the reading of these same verses by others.[22]

True, all may have been drawn by the same God through the same process of conviction and repentance to trust in Jesus as savior, but the imagination of each person represents a different mental journey in reaching the final destination. God provides "the subject matter and the impetus for our reasoning, our feelings, and our choices."[23] The power of his Spirit and the gift of our imaginations work in and through his word. For me, the words "I will give you rest" spoke to my deep longing to be free from the guilt of my sin, my personal failures, the emptiness of my heart, and my lack of satisfaction in my life. God used my imagination, in concert with his word, to bring me to my knees in repentance. On that day, I might well have been the only person moved in any way in that very full church.

As Veith and Ristuccia have helpfully reminded us, "imagination often provides the subject matter and the impetus for our reasoning, our feelings, and our choices."[24] And it is God-given! The imagination is also

---

22. Veith and Ristuccia, *Imagination Redeemed*, 142–43. Coincidentally, Matthew Ristuccia shares in his book that he too responded to Matthew 11:28–30. However, in his experience his attention as a keen birdwatcher was first captured by Matthew 6:26, which speaks of God caring for all of the birds of the air. When discussing this with a friend he was directed to Matthew 11, and he responded in faith to the promise of rest in Christ.

23. Ibid., 14.

24 Veith and Ristuccia, *Imagination Redeemed*, 14–15.

part of the way God takes over old selves and replaces and transforms them across our lives.[25]

Reason and the imagination of course work hand in hand. C. S. Lewis talked about the relationship between the imagination and reason this way:

> For me, reason is the natural organ of truth; but imagination is the organ of meaning. Imagination, producing new metaphors or revivifying old, is not the cause of truth, but its condition.[26]

In commenting on Lewis, Trevor Hart points to the way reason and imagination sit within the relationships of life as God is at work in us:

> What imagination supplies, Lewis suggests, is not just a cornucopia of material objects to be experienced, but the webs of relationships within which these objects are situated and in terms of which we are able to "make sense" of them.[27]

It is important to issue a final warning about the misuse of the imagination. As Veith and Ristuccia remind us,[28] God's word warns against the improper use of our imaginations. Scripture of course gives us guidance here. Jeremiah, for example, warns us not to walk "in the imagination of [our] hearts" (Jer 13:10). And, of course, Romans 1:21–23 reminds us that humankind in its endeavors can become darkened. Instead of being wise we become fools and exchange the glory of God for images of him made to look like mortals or even birds, animals, and reptiles. This is a case where human imagination is depraved and can lead away from God. Hence the quest of every Christian must be to "take captive every thought" and make them obedient to Christ (2 Cor 10:5).

As well, we must not allow discussions of the role of the imagination to displace the primary revelation of God through his word. While God only seeks to lead us toward truth, our imaginations, as well as our ignorance, can lead us elsewhere. Only when our imaginations are in step with the Spirit of God are we able to plumb the depths of God's wisdom that he reveals through his word.

However, we should not fear the imagination. As Hart reminds us,

---

25. Ibid., 31.
26. Lewis, "Bluspels and Flalansferes," 10–11.
27. Hart, *Between the Image and the Word*, 14.
28. Veith and Ristuccia, *Imagination Redeemed*, 13–16.

God, we may reasonably suppose, is just as capable of taking our imaginations captive as he is of engaging our "hearts," "minds" and "wills" . . . and may give himself to be known by appropriating human activities and outputs of a highly imaginative (as well as a relatively unimaginative) sort.[29]

Veith and Ristuccia nail home this point by linking the imagination and meaning more broadly in relation to life's goals:

The human imagination is where meaning is made, where a vision for life is set, where mind and heart and will converge. It is simultaneously the most strategic and the most forgotten part of the human soul when it comes to Christian discipleship.[30]

This process of our imaginations becoming redeemed and captive to the will of God is of course a lifelong one. It will remain unfinished even to the point of death. Like knowledge, skills, and abilities of varied kinds, imaginations are given to us in order to glorify God.[31] Our God reveals the purposes for which he created us, as we seek to cope and respond to life's experiences. He does this in parallel with our encounters with his revealed word. At God's initiative, he uses his word and our imaginations to convict, rebuke, and turn us from rebellion to acceptance of him as Lord and Savior.

IMAGINATION, PEDAGOGY, AND LEARNING

Having discussed what imagination is and how God uses it in our lives to draw us to himself, I want to discuss the role human imagination plays in our lives and that of the people we teach in varied contexts, including home, school, universities, and the church. I will do this by unpacking what I see as four key understandings that should shape why imagination is important to our pedagogy and how it might be sustained and promoted in our classrooms.

Imagination, Personhood, and Life

Human imagination is applied in varied ways, it reflects our personhood, and in turn is shaped as we engage imaginatively with the world. This

29. Hart, *Between the Image and the Word*, 41.

30. Ibid., 29–30.

31. Ibid., 30.

making of us in part reflects the stories and experiences we absorb and give expression to as we live as creative beings. We are not given our major focus and direction simply by reasoning, but also by the imagination. Our personalities and character are shaped by a life in which imagination and knowledge each play a part. Charles Taylor's work on the "social imaginary"[32] and James Smith's on the way we imagine our future discussed in chapter six are of course relevant to this point.[33]

To be human is to understand the God-given desire that primes our quest to understand our purpose and seek fulfillment in life. As we saw in chapter 7, this is partly expressed through the "intertextual cacophony of stories" that both stimulate our imaginations, and in turn are partly interpreted by our imaginations. As we encounter them, we seek to make sense of our world, and in turn, our desires and hopes are shaped and influenced by them.[34] The challenge for teachers and parents is how we cut across and channel this barrage of images, hopes, and desires.

As I mentioned earlier in the chapter, when Martin Buber spoke to the educational conference in 1925, he shocked the organizers by suggesting the conference theme that spoke of "development" of creativity was wrong, for this potential was present at birth! Like Hart[35] and others, he saw creativity as a gift of God to all. His argument was that all children are capable of imagination and the creativity that is related to it:

> Each child is born with a given disposition of "world-historical" origin, that is, inherited from the riches of the whole human race, and that he is born into a given situation of "world-historical" origin . . . In this as in every hour, what has not been invades the structure of what is . . . a creative event if ever there was one.[36]

Buber asserted every child begins life as an imaginative and creative being. At birth, all possesses an originator instinct which is autonomous and cannot be derived from others. Instead, he argued it simply needs cultivation.[37] While the school, church, preschool, or family can at times do their worst to snuff out this instinct, and while we might encourage and facilitate its use, we do not create it.

32. Taylor, *Modern Social Imaginaries.*

33. Smith, *Desiring the Kingdom.*

34. Cairney, "Intertextuality," 478–84.

35. Hart, *Between the Image and the Word,* 5.

36. Buber, *Between Man and Man,* 99–100.

37. Ibid., 100.

This precious disposition that we see in the newborn child, the three-year-old, or the mischievous eighty-year-old is nothing more or less than the capacity "to receive and imagine the world."[38]

While not denying that knowledge can be dispensed and learned, facts can be taught and discovered, skills demonstrated, explained, and hence acquired, the originator instinct requires the preservation of freedom expressed in communion. For it is freedom that in Buber's words will "open up," whereas "compulsion" creates disunion, humiliation, and rebelliousness. "Freedom in education is the possibility of [true] freedom."[39]

Imagination, Community, and Dialogue

As I have already mentioned above, the extent to which we engage the world with our imaginations has a strong relationship to the multiple communities in which we are dwellers. Imagination is critical to community-building, and in turn, communities can shape imaginations and how we use them. It is within communities of interest and practice that our view of the world, and our place within our multiple communities, are shaped. Inta's classroom, which I described in chapter 3, was just such an environment. The children, who shared and inspired one another, had a level of freedom to imaginatively explore their world. It is as we live among other people that our views, aspirations, goals, and hoped-for identities are shaped.

The Apostle Paul understood this as the early church emerged and people from varied backgrounds came together. In Ephesians 2 we read how Paul challenged this new community of believers to grasp that they were no longer bound by their past. They could seek a transformed life and live within a community where there was no longer Jew nor Greek, slave or free. Jew and Gentile alike needed to be able to imagine a new future, a new identity, and a new world, and in his letter to the church in Rome (6:11–13), he reminds them they could experience a new unity and standing before God, not shaped by their past.

Veith and Ristuccia suggest imagination expressed within community is an important way God transforms us. The imagination expressed, tested, and considered with others not only transforms individuals, it changes groups and builds communities. They cite the work of Brian Uzzi[40] to sup-

38. ibid., 104–7.
39. Ibid., 108.
40. Brian Uzzi is a globally recognized scientist, teacher, consultant, and speaker

port the point. Uzzi's work was based on an examination of the connection between friendship, collaboration, and creativity involved in more than two thousand staged musicals on Broadway. He found that the degree of friendship and social connectedness among people improved the performance.[41]

The imagination does not do as well in isolation; rather it is a community project.[42] The redeemed imagination will flourish more in relationship to other people who we not only know, but who we can trust. The teacher must grapple with the reality that in the classroom there may well be little that binds members together, little shared concern, or even a common hoped-for future. If this is the reality of the classroom, then the imaginations of the students will be exercised in pursuing other goals, hopes, and dreams. Inta's classroom and the proliferation of *Faraway Tree* stories also illustrates how one's work can be inspired and built upon, by others.

Maurice Friedman suggests

> the true teacher is not the one who pours information into the student's head as through a funnel—the old-fashioned "disciplined" approach—or the one who regards all potentialities as already existing within the student and needing to be pumped up—the newer "progressive" approach. It is the one who fosters genuine mutual contact and mutual trust, who experiences the other side of the relationship, and helps his pupils realize, through the selection of the effective world, what it can mean to be a man [*sic*].[43]

Any pedagogy that is worth considering involves the shaping of character. Friedman's words resonate strongly with our present condition as we struggle to enter into our students' worlds which seem so distant, ephemeral, and impenetrable.

Buber explored (amongst other things) the role of dialogue in human existence. He suggested speaking at one another is not conversation, and in fact communication might not include words at all. We can communicate much in our silence.[44]

---

on leadership, social networks, and new media. He is the Richard L. Thomas Professor of Leadership and Organizational Change at the Kellogg School of Management, Northwestern University.

41. Veith and Ristuccia, *Imagination Redeemed*, 135–36.

42. Ibid., 136.

43. Friedman, "Introduction," xvii–xviii.

44. Buber, *Between Man and Man*, 3–5.

The key to reducing the generational distance between teacher and child, and to establishing classrooms and schools as communities that are transformative, would seem to be a better understanding of one another. Teachers need to consider how they perceive their students. Do teachers spend their time in classrooms as observers and onlookers? Or have they formed communities of learners and an environment in which they are able to speak into the lives of their students. Conversely, how do their students see them? When I speak of communities of learners in this book I am speaking of more than a group of people in a classroom learning together. I am suggesting we need to form and support relational communities where members do more than listen and observe. We need to create contexts where they can speak into our lives as well. John Collier has been a leader for reform in Australian Christian education, and worked closely with Trevor Cooling, a leader in the United Kingdom Christian schools sector.[45] Collier suggests we "must allow students space to think, and indeed encourage critical thinking." Furthermore, we must open opportunities for dialogue in our classrooms. He writes wisely,

> Didactic transmission of the content of Christian faith is unlikely to resonate well with current youth. A more interactive and engaging manner is likely to achieve better student commitment than resorting simply to narrative teaching styles.[46]

The distance between teacher and student is little more than a relational artefact. A classroom where there is compliance, where students do their work and perhaps even achieve highly, is not necessarily a transformative classroom. We must ask what groups and communities are providing the relational contexts that are speaking into your students' lives.

How is this discussion of dialogue and relational communities connected to imagination? It is a foundational part of how such communities are formed. Imagination is central to how our student minds are engaged, hopes are formed, aspirations are primed, friendships are conceived, and supported. As students engage in the life of the school and the communities of practice they inhabit, imagination plays a key role in connecting who they are, who they wish to become, and what is critical to their sense of belonging.

---

45. Goodlet and Collier, *Teaching Well.*
46. Collier, "Models of Christian Education," 7.

Imagination, Identity, and Learning

As our students arrive in our schools and classrooms, they do not come as clean slates. Instead, they come with memories and hopes, and imagination is related to both. The new and novel event or experience can trigger the imagination, and drive us to respond. As we discussed in chapter 7, children are immersed in story and engage and interact with their world from birth. Their knowledge of the world and their place within it are distilled from a limitless array of experiences, stories, and memories. The memory of the past always has an impact on the shaping of our futures. Our imaginations play a key role in interpreting the present, remembering and making sense of our past, and defining our hopes for the future. In fact, the imagination doesn't simply shape how we see ourselves as children. Paul Ricoeur wrote extensively on the role of the imagination in faith and suggested it can also help us to build new identities, indeed, even "redemption through imagination."[47]

Our experiences and memories in concert with our imaginations can take us in many directions. Some of our memories can lead to a range of human emotions including pride, bitterness, lust, anger, even regret. But God can take our memories captive as well as our imaginations. Veith and Ristuccia talk of the redeemed imagination as a "righteous imagination." In explaining what they mean by this, they suggest we need to understand our "imagination feed." They describe this as "the network of visual or mental input, behaviors, relationships, and unopposed ruminating thoughts that feed your imagination." In essence, they suggest how we feed the imagination, and what we feed it with, has a direct relationship to whether our imagination is corrupted or redeemed.[48] This is a critical insight for teachers in the age of social media and short attention spans.

Richard Hays offers insights that might help in this challenge as he too considers the key role of the imagination. He says of Paul,

> In 1 Corinthians, we find Paul calling his readers and hearers to a conversion of the imagination. He was calling Gentiles to understand their identity anew in light of the gospel of Jesus Christ—a gospel message comprehensible only in relation to the larger narrative of God's dealing with Israel.[49]

47. Ricoeur, "The Image of God and the Epic of Man," 127.
48. Veith and Ristuccia, *Imagination Redeemed*, 105–6.
49. Hays, *The Conversion of the Imagination*, 5.

Jews and Gentiles were being challenged by the gospel to reevaluate their identities. Such a profound shift in perspective, so profound that our very imaginations are captured, requires reason, memory, and the imagination as the Spirit of God transforms us. As Hays argues, this transformation in the early church was achieved as Paul constantly fostered and sustained this "by a process of bringing the community's beliefs and practices into critical confrontation with the gospel story." This understanding has been at the heart of much of what we have discussed in the last three chapters. In many ways, what we seek in our classrooms and schools is what Hays calls a "conversion of the imagination."[50]

Ricoeur offers an insight into how this might occur in suggesting "the imagination generates new metaphors for synthesizing disparate aspects of reality that burst conventional assumptions about the nature of things."[51] He foresaw this happening as our presuppositions are challenged through the work of the imagination, and as we connect experiences and understandings to generate metaphors that make sense of how we see the world. Ricoeur saw our imaginations as assisting understanding and even matters of faith. As we encounter life, and have hopes dashed and at times realized, the use of imagination through metaphor helps us make sense of our state of being and imagine other possibilities. A key question for all Christian teachers is how might we create contexts in which our students' imaginations can be transformed? I will return to this question later in the chapter as well as in chapter 9.

Walter Brueggemann also points to the role of the imagination in opening our eyes to new insights. He reminds us that engaging the imagination through story and poetry was the major mode of education in ancient Israel. First, because they are concrete and able to locate people, places, times, and events, but also, because they are open-ended in the sense that they can be told in varied forms and genres without changing the content. They were intended for the "practice of imagination" and required the listener to supply effort to understand. Brueggemann suggests this was a shared practice of a "secret which evokes imagination." Stories for the Israelites were also experiential, detailing what happened, and what was seen and heard. Finally, the story was seen as having its own power to teach about the reality of their experience.[52] This he suggests is as God had

50. Ibid., x.
51. Ibid., 8.
52. Brueggemann, *The Creative Word*, 22–27.

intended in the prophetic poetry that we read in the Bible. This he suggests was given to us by God "to take Israel inside the life experiences which might be treated externally as only ethical or political."[53]

Christian parents and teachers also use story and imagination as key tools to share biblical truth. In the telling, there is always an attempt to capture imaginations and invite each child into the story being told. The aim is to help them see themselves in the story, to imagine Jesus healing the sick, raising the dead, freeing the captives, and so on. This is a carefully orchestrated sharing designed to make them attentive to details, be challenged by the surprising, and imagine how God is exercising grace, mercy, and love in their lives.

Imagination, Reading, and the Word

As discussed earlier in the chapter, the imagination is a gift from God. He made us to know and worship him and built into us the capacity to imagine the future and to try to make sense of the past. He created us as beings who are able to use language and think in metaphors, creatures who could also create and respond to their world and condition in language, including poetic forms. He made us able to create images and other representations of meaning, and with the desire to search for meaning in the world he gave to us.

As imagining creatures, God draws us to himself. Nowhere is our imagination more important than in helping us understand the depth of meaning of God's word to us spoken by the prophets, teachers, disciples, and of course through his Son.

Richard Hays suggests we can learn a great deal more about the use of the imagination to understand our world, as well as the Bible, which is God's word to us. But how can we read God's word in ways that illuminate the depth of meaning embedded in it? Hays suggests that in the Apostle Paul we see someone who demonstrates that "he reads Scripture narratively," not simply as a historian or systematic theologian, but as a poetic preacher looking for correspondences between story in Scripture and the gospel he proclaims in spoken word as well as in his letters. Paul, he suggests, seeks to grasp the depth of meaning in God's word.[54]

53. Ibid., 53.
54. Hays, *The Conversion of the Imagination*, xvi.

Hays offers us a picture of a reader we need to understand and embrace as we encourage our children to understand the mystery of God's word. He suggests Paul is a "provocative reader" of Scripture, who displays "powerful imaginative readings" as he interprets God's word.[55] As Paul writes and speaks, he invites us to be provocative readers too, challenging us to seek and proclaim God's kingdom. This is not to suggest Paul's words are mere creations of his own. Rather, his words reflect his imaginative, as well as intellectual, reading of Scripture, and his communication of God's truth to hearers and readers. This imagination, Hays argues, is a gift from God that enables us to grasp what it is God communicates to us.

One of Paul Ricoeur's major contributions was to stress how hermeneutics involves the relationship between the self and symbols. Imagination plays a key part in the intertextual relationship between the memories, experience, and imaginations of life with words, images, and experiences. An understanding of oneself, as well as life's purpose and our imagined future, are the outcomes of such an intertextual tapestry of life experiences.

As my final word on the topic of the imagination, I want to return to my earlier comments on the way C. S. Lewis saw truth and the imagination. Hopefully, in this chapter we have seen that imagination is a gift of God to humanity, and that reason and the imagination have a relationship to one another. As Lewis suggested,

> For me, reason is the natural organ of truth; but imagination is the organ of meaning. Imagination, producing new metaphors or revivifying old, is not the cause of truth, but its condition.[56]

It is worth emphasizing that while imagination can indeed help us seek and gain truth, it is not a requirement for this to occur. Truth is not a fanciful, individual creation, and is never relative.

The imagination is a gift from God for life and indeed is part of the way he draws us to himself. Anthony Esolen has a delightful way of expressing the tension between what we know and what we do not know and have yet to discover:

> The imagination opens out not principally to what it knows and finds familiar, but to what it does not know, what it finds strange, half hidden, robed with inaccessible light.[57]

55. Ibid., xvi.
56. Lewis, "Bluspels and Flalansferes," 10–11.
57. Esolen, *Ten Ways to Destroy the Imagination of Your Child*, 221.

This of course, is why stimulating the imaginations of our children is so critical. In chapter 9, I will return to imagination as I bring the threads and arguments of this book together and outline a framework for pedagogy.

9

A Framework for Evaluating Classroom and School Life

Education worthy of its name is essentially education of character. For the genuine educator does not merely consider individual functions of his pupils, as one intending to teach him only to know or be capable of certain things; but his concern is always the person as a whole, both in the actuality in which he lives before you now and in the possibilities, what he can become.[1]

—MARTIN BUBER

APPLYING BIBLICAL UNDERSTANDING TO A RIGHT PEDAGOGY

We have covered much ground in this book. First, we considered what pedagogy is and isn't, with a concern for human formation central to our discussions. The two dual themes of pedagogy and formation have been woven throughout all chapters. This included the very first chapter on pedagogy, and later chapters that have looked at learning, the development of classroom life, story, and the imagination. My primary task has been to consider how pedagogy relates to teaching, learning, community, formation, and faith. In doing this we have also considered the central role of story in communities of practice, and the role of the imagination as the intellectual activity of the mind that connects prior and new knowledge and experiences. Imagination is part of the way we make sense of, and

1. Buber, *Between Man and Man*, 123.

respond to, our world. It is also implicated in identity, learning, language, and creativity. Now we need to consider what the broad central indicators or markers of Christian pedagogy are in the life of the Christian school.

It is important to remind readers, this book was never going to end with a suggested curriculum, nor key methods to be followed. Rather, my intent was always to share a view of pedagogy consistent with an intent to help young people to live with a focus on the kingdom. This is a view of schooling in which I have defined education as "the whole of life of a community, and the experience of its members learning to live this life together, from the standpoint of a specific end goal." I have argued throughout that there is freedom to choose alternative teaching methods, a vast array of curriculum materials, and programs from school to school within the mandated requirements of government curricula. In this chapter I provide a pedagogical framework I believe is consistent with a biblical view of the purpose and intent of Christian education, that is, education centered on the formation of character and a faith that sees hope for our future in God, not in one's achievements and pride in our human qualities. As Martin Buber suggests in the quote that heads this chapter, "Education worthy of its name is essentially education of character." This education of character involves the "person as a whole" and education and the teacher as "their vehicle."[2]

Our students need to be resilient people who live in the world, but who have an understanding of an eternal world, and know their ultimate hopes and desires are to be gained in and through a life lived for God. Our pedagogy must be one that considers the whole child and their orientation to the kingdom of God.

As I have argued in previous chapters, the intent in opening up the richness and depth of student lives to the teacher is critical to formation. Only by understanding students' worlds and something of the varied communities of practice they inhabit, will teachers be able to influence their formation beyond mere compliance and assent. If superficial assent is all we achieve in education, behavior might move towards compliance, but as teachers we will have limited access to their varied worlds.

Instead, our hope is we might create an openness within our students, allowing windows to be opened into their lives, including their hopes, dreams, and desires so they might come under the transformative power of the gospel.

2. Ibid., 120.

In chapter 6, I suggested we needed an attentiveness to the student life of the classroom to create opportunities to observe their actions, emotions, hopes, fears, frustrations, and joys. One of my colleagues in the field of education, Professor Yetta Goodman, coined the term "kidwatching" for teachers of young children.[3] Her aim was to encourage teachers to watch and collect "data" and act on it. At its most basic level, kidwatching requires teachers to use their eyes to observe student lives, and their ears to listen to what students do and don't say, not in order to judge, or to indoctrinate, but to understand them. We need to demonstrate a desire to come to a greater understanding of why our students do or do not engage in activities within the classroom and school. In the case of Chanda, whom we met in chapter 2, what I did was not startling. First, I acted on her noncompliance with the writing curriculum when I observed it. Second, I asked some questions. Finally, I took the time to observe her more closely, and I made an effort to know her better. This deliberate activity made a difference.

Similarly, what characterized Inta's classroom work we discussed in chapter 3 were her key pedagogical assumptions about learning, teaching, and curriculum. These had an impact on shaping her practices in classroom management, use of space, forms of interaction permitted, rules for conduct, access to resources, interaction patterns, and so on. She was highly organized, with a clear structure to her day, defined class rules for behavior, and well-identified expectations. Her teaching technique was strong, her curriculum knowledge was deep, and her intent was high. All of this of course was influenced by her faith, and the desire she had for all her students to know her God and have their lives shaped by the knowledge of him.

The pedagogy that was demonstrated in each of these vignettes was consistent with the definition of education outlined in chapter 1, and addressed in the first half of the book. At the foundation of what I have been arguing so far is a belief that a right view of God and our relationship to him should be foundational to Christian educational pedagogy. In the rest of the chapter I highlight what I see as the key dimensions to such a pedagogy. This is not meant to be a comprehensive framework, or prescriptive recipe for classroom action; this is impossible in the cut and thrust of day-to-day teaching. Classrooms are messy places, teachers are fallible and different, and the complexity of life of the school will mean what we are talking about

3. Owocki and Goodman, *Kidwatching.*

is no more than ensuring our best efforts are well-informed as we seek to transform classroom life over time.

The start of good Christian pedagogy will be the teacher's mirroring of the person of Christ to make good and wise choices as they nurture their children. As a teacher, I know this will require making different (though hopefully consistent) decisions for each child in our care. It will also require us to respond in different ways, and offer different forms of support, each and every day. It is important to stress that if we search for the perfect pedagogy, we will have a fruitless search, for the day-to-day working out of our pedagogy will vary from teacher to teacher and class to class. But—and this is an important "but"—we should strive to teach in ways that are true to the way God has created us and his purposes for doing so. We must constantly acknowledge our nature as learners and creatures made in the image of God, and the essence of community shaped by the gospel of Christ.

It needs to be said that in the minutiae of decisions to be made for each child and every new situation, there is freedom for teachers to make different choices. This particularly relates to the methods teachers use, the way errors are corrected, how learning is promoted and supported, and of course the way initiative and learning are encouraged. This is where what we have learned about the nature of learners, child development, and educational theory is important and relevant. As educators, we must discern what is right and wise, and not simply accept the latest fad or whim of other educational experts. Our thinking should always be informed by what God teaches us in his word, which of course shapes our worldview. This in turn can inform and influence our thinking and action.[4]

The great challenge for teachers and leaders in Christian schools is to consider what should be distinctive about our education and schooling. As Professor John McDowell argues, the application of theology to education requires us to see theology as an "education in good judgment, or that which involves the shaping of discerning practice by good vision."[5] This, he argued, requires consideration of many things, including "responsive attention" to the subject matter, concern for community, and a willingness to question and critique.

---

4. Beech, *Christians as Teachers*, 62. Many books have been written about worldview, but far too often they end up prescribing a worldview framework for curriculum and method. As a result, they end up spending more time discussing what we believe and little time considering pedagogy. This book is a rare exception and offers a balanced treatment of worldview thinking and other key issues.

5. McDowell, "The Future of Theology," 19.

Good pedagogy is the key to the creation of a classroom or school that has a Christian distinctive. When I visit schools that have a reputation for being outstanding Christian institutions, I always observe collaborative learning communities that allow teachers to work together within the limits of their God-given abilities. Together, they construct contexts that enable human flourishing and open minds and a willingness and desire to understand how others see the world and why. As we work as teachers, we help our students understand how we live the way God intended. As Christian schools, this must be informed by a faith grounded in Christ and sound doctrines shaped by our understanding of God and his plans for us. As Geoff Beech argues, it is important not to use the Bible selectively to justify our practices. Rather, teachers need to know the Bible well and read it "as God's story and not only selecting verses or small passages that we happen to relate to well or that fit our sense of what is normal in the Christian life and belief."[6]

The framework in Table 1 had its genesis as part of my contribution to the Anglican Education Forum I mentioned in chapter 2, and was included in a different form in an earlier publication.[7] Since then, I have revised, rethought, and expanded the thinking that shaped the framework. This, in part, has reflected conversations and interactions with schoolteachers and educators. In schools, there is a desire to consider pedagogy seriously in the light of biblical understanding, as well as educational research and writing.

I have organized the discussion of the framework under three major headings, which reflect the theology that has informed the whole book, as well as the biblical theology of personhood that was described in chapter 4. Three broad biblical truths give shape to the framework: "God is Creator," "God's creatures are meant to be learners," and "God made us for communion." The discussion of the framework follows, but it is also included in Table 1 as a series of statements. The question form is designed to invite discussion among colleagues as they tussle with the challenge to understand what Christian education means in their educational context, and what it might become in the future.

6. Beech, *Christians as Teachers*, 63.

7. Cairney et al., *New Perspectives in Anglican Education*.

A FRAMEWORK FOR CHRISTIAN PEDAGOGY

God made us as unique creatures

1. Identify that which is valuable in each child.
2. Build on the foundations of the family.
3. Demonstrate and encourage service.
4. Develop a right view of work and effort.

[handwritten annotation: compassion, grace]

God made us as creatures who learn

5. Develop meaning-makers who interpret language and knowledge to know "truth."
6. Develop humble learners.
7. Understand the diverse nature of learners, and identify and respond to individual needs.
8. Create opportunities for students to take responsibility for learning.
9. Foster the development of imagination and creativity.
10. Encourage creative risk-taking and problem-solving.
11. Utilize varied methods to facilitate learning in diverse learners.
12. Act as kidwatchers, observing and monitoring student learning and well-being.
13. Evaluate the ends toward which our pedagogy is directed.
14. Make our classrooms places where just punishment and discipline are evident.

God made us for communion

15. Demonstrate forgiveness and seek repentance in students as hearts are trained.
16. Model and promote self-sacrifice and generosity.
17. Seek and model justice within class and school community life.
18. Ensure learning in the classroom is related to the world beyond.
19. Promote the importance of story in your classroom and school.
20. Implement pedagogical practices that demonstrate a relationship between education and discipleship.

A FRAMEWORK FOR CHRISTIAN PEDAGOGY

If you read through the framework alone, I encourage you to answer the questions and make notes. You might consider using a technique I developed many years ago called "Talk to the Author."[8] This technique was designed to help engage my students as they read, in order to increase the depth of their reading and comprehension. Its purpose is to encourage you to engage and reflect on the implications of the questions in the framework. You might also wish to discuss the questions and your answers with a colleague or two. Within groups I would encourage open dialogue, questioning, and challenge as you reveal your thoughts on pedagogy and seek to grow in shared knowledge of the arguments supporting the framework.

God's Unique Creatures

1. Do I identify that which is valuable in each child?
The Bible teaches that all people are made in the image of God (Gen 1:26) and are the objects of his love and forgiveness. Teachers and students within Christian schools are to demonstrate the God-given ability to see that which is precious in all people. God loves us all, and in his eyes there are no favorites. So too with Christian teachers. The challenge we face is to look for that which is good in every student. This might be difficult at times, so pray for your students and your relationship with them.

2. Do my class and school build on the foundations of the family?
God made us to live in relationship first with him, and second with other people. The family was the foundation of humanity (Gen 2:15–25), and continues to be the foundation for learning in the early years of life (Deut 6:1–9). It also has a vital role throughout schooling. Hence, part of the responsibility of the Christian school is to know the families of our students, and to support them as they nurture their children and as God works in their lives. Families are not problems to be managed, but rather partners in education and recipients of God's grace, sometimes delivered through the school. I have discussed the role of parents throughout this book, but it might be worth revisiting some of these comments in chapters 1 to 3 concerning the key partnership we have with families.

8. Cairney, *Teaching Reading Comprehension*, 72–75.

3. How do your classroom and school demonstrate and encourage service to one another?

God made us to commune with him and one another; we are to contribute to each other and seek the good of the community, not just the self (Matt 22:37–40). Hence, teachers and all school leaders seek to act in ways that foster community by encouraging all members to serve one another in word and action. The teacher in God's service is an example to their students, just as they are an example to one another. Service and servanthood should be the mark of all teachers and of central importance to any classroom within a Christian school. God the Servant King made us to be servants to him, but also to one another.[9] Jesus, of course, is the perfect example of service, having given his life for us (Phil 2:7; Matt 20:25–28). Our example is a critical part of what it is to be a Christian teacher, as we demonstrate what service looks like, as well as shepherding and watching over them, always showing eagerness to serve them and "be examples to the flock" (1 Pet 5:3).

4. Do our practices reflect a right view of work and effort?

God made us to contribute to the order and running of his world in our work (Gen 2:15). Work is reflective of God's plan for us, and as such is part of what it means to be human. There is also an instrumental aspect to work; it is a means to some end. And yes, work can be hard as we toil, but it can also bring good and glorify God. Related to this is the place of rest and how we model this for our children and the way the life of the school is structured and priorities set.

Christians are to embrace and view their work as good and part of God's plan. Therefore, our attitude is to be one of gratefulness that God has given us work to do, and we are to encourage our students to adopt similar attitudes. Hard work is not to be shunned or complained about, but embraced as part of life. No matter how difficult teaching can be, how menial or boring some tasks might seem—like marking, playground duty, staff meetings, and so on—our work as teachers offers opportunity for fellowship with our God in the midst of the good days and the bad. Our God is always with us. As he told Israel through the prophet Isaiah, "So do not fear, for I am with you; do not be dismayed, for I am your God. I will

---

9. David Starling in his excellent book on Christian leadership reminds us that "*all good leadership takes the form of 'servant-leadership.'*" Starling, *Uncorinthian Leadership*, 9–10.

strengthen you and help you; I will uphold you with my righteous right hand" (Isa 41:10). Fellowship with God is possible in any circumstance of life, including work.

God's Creatures as Learners

5. Do our students as learners demonstrate an ability to interpret language and knowledge to know "truth?"

God made us as meaning-makers to know him, and to learn by and from the truth of his word. Christian pedagogy requires an understanding of how knowledge is created, known, and shared. Our students need a deep knowledge of language, and how its meanings can be tested. They must also have an ability to interpret language. Life is filled with meaning-making, and the quest for knowledge is to be valued by placing a priority on the gaining, sharing, and testing of knowledge and truth. Ultimately, it is God's truth that needs to be discerned as we seek true freedom and the fulfillment of God's purposes (John 8:31–33). A love of learning and language is vital to knowledge. To seek truth is the most appropriate response to a God who has given us the great gifts of learning and discernment. Mike Higton goes even further in connecting truth and learning to suggest "all learning worthy of the name—is a matter of being invited as disciples to know God and the fulfilment that God has for God's creatures."[10] Such learning, he argues, takes place in and outside the church. Understanding God and his purposes in and through Christ is foundational to true learning. All else, while still part of our human existence in the world, is of secondary value and is subject to true learning.

6. Do we seek to develop humble learners?

God made us as creatures who learn (Prov 1:5, 9:9, 22:6; Deut 6:4–9). Such learning is always known by God. There is nothing that is not known by him, and so humility is needed by all learners, as well as an understanding that our achievements are ultimately for the glory of God, not the self, the teacher, or the school. How we acknowledge success and achievement should always be framed by our knowledge that God is to be praised in all things. This will include encouraging cooperation between learners,

10. Higton, *A Theology of Higher Education*, 145.

and generosity in the way resources, knowledge, and skills are shared with others.[11]

7. Do we understand the diverse nature of learners and identify as well as respond to individual needs?

Since God made us to be different, we will have different strengths, weaknesses, and needs (Rom 12:6). Teachers, classrooms, and schools should demonstrate this understanding in word and action. We should seek to respond to, value, and respect our children's varied needs and gifts. Teaching to the middle, or application of restrictive methods to the point of frustration for some, is not an option that should serve as a goal or acceptable practice. We are to encourage and help students who are slower to learn, and enrich those students who show specific gifts. With an understanding that God has gifted us in varying ways, we must seek to educate for all.

As well, our acceptance of difference must extend to social harmony among our students. In the tradition of *shalom*, we are to seek the flourishing of all in our care. Our children come to us each day with varied gifts, lived experiences, ethnicities, abilities, and pasts. On any day, we will have troubled children in our classrooms. As Jesus neared the crucifixion, he said, "Peace I leave with you; my peace I give you. I do not give to you as the world gives. Do not let your hearts be troubled and do not be afraid" (John 14:27). Safety and the assurance of physical needs was not what Jesus was promising. *Shalom* meant much more than this. While *shalom* can mean tranquility and peace in the sense of freedom from harm, it also means unity and accord among people. While true spiritual harmony involves restoration with God, Christian classrooms must be places that demonstrate *shalom* in the sense of harmony within the community, peace among students, love and service to one another, and a culture of restoration of differences with others. Higton, as he discusses Wolterstorff's[12] work on *shalom*,

11. As an aside, Christians should not assume only they can act pedagogically in ways that honor God and fulfill God's plan for our lives. This goes to the heart of how Christian schools structure curriculum, appoint staff, choose literature, and select student leaders. If the Christian school is to be a place of formation and training in discipleship for those children from Christian homes, and indeed the smaller number who are believers in Christ, it must also be a place where we recognize God at work in the lives of every student and staff member. All people are God's creation. All are capable of displaying aspects of the Christlike life. Calvin, as we know, spoke of "common grace." God is always at work in all. Mike Higton suggests that the shared life of students and teachers should be "shaped by humility, and above all, by friendship." Ibid., 20.

12. Wolterstorff, *Educating for Shalom*.

suggests institutions that seek *shalom* "educate for the peacable kingdom of God" and "find delight in living rightly before God."[13]

8. Do we create opportunities for students to take responsibility for learning?

While teachers must exercise authority over their students, and students in turn must learn to respect the authority of their teachers, self-responsibility should be nurtured. Our God is sovereign and constrains the very hearts of his people through his Spirit, but he also allows freedom for his creatures to act. We are to nurture self-responsibility, wise judgment, and a desire to learn and act responsibly for right reasons (1 Cor 6:12). There are appropriate and inappropriate things to do in any school. The concept of freedom in our classrooms must be carefully understood. There is no justification, in the interest of human flourishing, for letting our students do anything they like. Schools like Summerhill, as originally established by A. S. Neill[14] in 1921, place a priority on giving students total freedom without restraint, and with autonomous self-responsibility. This is not a model suggested by the Scriptures. While we seek the development of self-responsibility in our children, we do not seek to achieve it by removing all rules and restraints.

The Bible's idea of freedom is that it is a freedom of conscience. No person is truly free until Jesus Christ has rid him or her of the burden of his guilt (Rom 6:20–23). Some of you may well remember the first time you moved away from home. You may have felt a sense of freedom, doing things that parents might have seen as unwise or even wrong. Were you free? Well, yes, free from your parents. But were you truly free? Talk to non-Christian friends and you will see that the image of Christianity today is not freedom but bondage. Our task as Christian teachers is to help our students grasp a biblical understanding of freedom in the life of the school. Christians are not the fun police, and Christianity is not a religion of don'ts.[15]

Thomas Chalmers (a leader of the Free Church of Scotland) was correct back in the nineteenth century when he talked about the "expulsive power of a new affection." That is to say, if you want to get rid of a sin, you

---

13. Higton, *A Theology of Higher Education*, 119.

14. Neill, *Summerhill School*.

15. We can go to many places in the Bible for help on freedom, including Galatians 5, Romans 6, John 8, and 1 Peter 2. It is much more than just avoiding things, it is also about choosing positively for righteousness.

don't replace it with a vacuum—you replace it with an even stronger passion for something good.[16] In chapter 6, we considered the work of James Smith who reminded us that our desires are aimed at specific ends or goals, and set the trajectory for our lives. "A vision of the good life captures our hearts and imaginations."[17] So if our students are addicted to Facebook, there is no point in replacing it with WhatsApp—this simply replaces one type of social media with another. True change—and true freedom—requires a new allegiance.

9. Do we foster the development of the imagination and creativity?

God made us to be imaginative beings with varied skills that we are to teach to others. Our imaginative natures are used by God in our lives and as part of our worship of and search for him. It is at least partly through our imaginations and longings that we seek God and he seeks us. The purpose is that we might know him and experience all he intended for us. God's revelation of himself, including his truth and purposes for us, can involve his use of our imagination (Rev 22:1–21; Eph 1:17–18). Do we create classroom and school environments in which the imagination is celebrated and enjoyed as an essential part of the flourishing of human beings as knowing animals? Do we also encourage imaginative interest in learning about God's world and his purposes, and creative applications of the knowledge and gifts he has given to us? We should! This topic was discussed in full in chapter 8.

10. Do we encourage creative risk-taking and problem-solving in all learners?

God delights in his creation, the work of his hands and the sharing of these gifts with others (Exod 35:30–35). So too, he calls us to work in the world he has given us with a view to the future. In Genesis 1 man is given the tasks of "filling," "subduing," and having "dominion" over the earth (Gen 1:26–28). This does not mean simply the function of maintenance, but also of developing, cultivating, and making so creation continues to move ultimately toward its end. God's world is simultaneously in a state of decay and recreation. He calls us to use creative minds and willing hands to develop and sustain the world until his kingdom comes (2 Cor 5:1–21). Do

---

16. Chalmers was a Scottish preacher (1780–1847). In this famous sermon, he preached passionately on the need to replace the affections of the world with the love of Christ. Chalmers, "The Expulsive Power of a New Affection," n.p.

17. James Smith, *Desiring the Kingdom*, 53.

we nurture and place value on the development of curiosity and creativity as we encourage students to act in and on the world as they await the return of Jesus?

Martin Buber suggests that "the world, that is the whole environment, nature and society, 'educates' the human being: it draws out his powers, and makes him grasp and penetrate its objections."[18] The teacher is to create a "world" in which children see problems to be solved, opportunities to puzzle over life matters, and the "strangeness" of the world as they seek to make their way in it as risk-taking and problem-solving learners.

11. Do we utilize varied methods to facilitate learning in diverse learners?

God delights in us as learners and has given us the ability to learn in varied ways. Learning can occur in formal and informal ways (Deut 6:1–9), and draw on varied methods including observation and experience (Luke 13:18–21), parables (Ezek 17; Luke 8:4–8), allegories (Isa 5:1–7; Ezek 16), first-hand experience (Luke 9:1–8; 10:1–20), discussion and questioning (Luke 24:13–25), signs and symbolic acts (1 Kgs 11:29–39; Isa 20:1–6), and direct expository teaching through the spoken and written word. Do we exercise our freedom to use sound and varied methods that equip our students for the whole of life?

Just as we know there are many methods in teaching, there are many different types of learners. Indeed, God made us as individuals, no two of us are exactly the same (1 Cor 12:27). As well, he gave to each of us gifts. The Apostle Peter reminds us that each of us "should use whatever gift you have received to serve others, as faithful stewards of God's grace in its various forms." (1 Pet 4:10).

Since our students are so diverse, we will need to vary our teaching practices to suit their varied needs and giftings.

12. Are we kidwatchers, constantly observing and monitoring our students' learning, well-being, and journey toward faith?

As I have discussed earlier in this chapter, if we are to influence the life of our classrooms, we need to be engaged with our students and conscious of the day-to-day life of our classrooms. This includes life outside the classroom, which always has an impact on life within our schools. How aware are we of the behavior of our students outside the classroom? If they are

18. Buber, *Between Man and Man*, 106.

demonstrating inappropriate behavior in other places, how might we use this to inform how we get to know them and help them to adopt a different focus in their lives? What about their life at home? Do they come to school hungry, untidy, without resources, homework, and so on? What is our relationship with their parents like? Do we know them at all? Do we have any idea what passions and interests our students have outside school? How can we build on what we know about our children to encourage them and form them? Do we listen to them as they arrive and leave, play and chat with friends in informal moments, in order to gain insight into the multiple communities of practice they inhabit? Do we ask open questions that invite response, offering a window into the hearts and minds of our students?

Earlier in this chapter, I spoke of kidwatching and the need to understand the richness of students' lives. Do we demonstrate a desire to come to a greater understanding of why our students do or don't engage in the activities within the classroom and school? Only by listening, observing, and asking the right questions will we know our students more fully and be able to assess their well-being and journeys toward faith.

13. Do we actively evaluate the ends toward which our pedagogy is directed?

Perhaps the greatest challenge we face in seeking to create authentic Christian education is the negotiation of right purposes for learning. The *telos* of learning in our culture is rarely based on the desire for virtue or faith (although some will accept that it might be an outcome). Rather, most parents value material success and the attainment of power and influence. Do our schools simply adopt the same stance and seek the same priorities? How do we respond to and inform the expectations of our parents? We should continue to evaluate our attitudes and priorities that shape what we do, and the emphasis we give to certain things. Are the things we do pointing our children toward the good? Or are we distracted primarily by the values of the world? This is a tricky area. What shapes our view of the future? The following questions might serve as a helpful way to discuss these issues with colleagues.

a. Do we have a right balance in our projected purpose and vision for our class?

b. What do the stories we tell about ourselves signal in terms of our priorities?

c. What posture do we adopt toward success and the way we define it?

    d.   What are the expectations we project to parents?

    e.   If we are in leadership and appoint staff, how do we assess their view of the purpose of schooling and its end goal?

14. Are our classrooms places where just punishment and discipline are part of school life?

Proverbs 13:24 teaches that he who loves the child "is diligent to discipline him," but such punishment is to be just and not in anger and for revenge. Do we understand that unjust and unexplained punishment, punishment that breaks the spirit or is in anger and frustration, is wrong? Do we see punishment and discipline as a means that "yields the peaceful fruit of righteousness to those who have been trained by it" (Heb 12:11)? And through discipline, do we also show our love and concern?

Any kind of physical punishment is banned in most Western countries; hence discipline is inevitably related to detention, spoken comments, the withdrawal of privileges, and the involvement of parents. However, while some will see limted options for punishment, sound teaching requires management of classroom life in such a way that punishment is rarely needed. If our students are motivated and encouraged to contribute positively to community life, and are engaged in the activities of the classroom and school, discipline usually becomes less necessary. Having said this, if punishment is required, it must be applied fairly, consistently, and justly.

God Made Us for Communion

15. How do we demonstrate forgiveness and seek repentance in students as hearts are trained?

The Bible teaches that all have sinned and fall short of the glory of God (Rom 3:23), and one day will face judgment (Matt 12:36; John 16:8; 2 Cor 5:10). Do we demonstrate that we know all are in need of forgiveness and redemption? Do teachers, classrooms, and schools articulate and reinforce this understanding in the way they deal with sin in the lives of students?

Some of the greatest lessons in life are acquired in the midst of disappointment, failure, and distress. How Christian teachers deal with such opportunities for learning is very important. Being able to forgive and restore relationships within the classroom is one of the great skills of the outstanding teacher. How we relate to parents at such times is also very important.

Training and encouraging students to forgive one another is an important part of the work teachers do.

16. Does my classroom model and promote self-sacrifice and generosity?
God's ultimate purposes for us are that we know him, love him, serve him, and bring glory to him (1 Cor 10:31). Do our words and actions as teachers and school communities demonstrate where our hope is in life? Do we encourage our children to imitate Jesus in service, self-sacrifice, and generosity towards others? Is this the basis of community in the Christian school?

In the education world, competition seems to be expected, and is a key means to promote effort. Seeking to do well and to succeed is not wrong, but if it becomes an unhealthy obsession, where our students need to win and succeed at any cost, we know their efforts are wrongly motivated. To do well is good, but to do so simply to be better than others is not. How we encourage our students to have a right attitude toward success at school and to seek God's glory, not our own, is an important matter for all teachers. Our students need to be encouraged to support other students who need help, to be humble when they do better than others, and to be generous in how they contribute to group projects and non-individual assignments and activities. Whether participating in academic, sporting, cultural, or community service activities, we should encourage our students to support the work and efforts of others, not just our own.

17. Is justice in God's world sought and modeled within class and school community life?
Our God is just, and his justice is an expression of his holiness. Hence, God expects his people to seek justice in the world and demonstrate it (Mic 6:8). Is this seen in the way justice is delivered within the school community and through the curriculum? Do the curriculum and the attitude of teachers show a concern for the world?

Classrooms must be places turned towards the world and aware of the inequities and injustices within it. How do we demonstrate kindness to others and actively promote compassionate hearts in our students? Do we encourage empathy and respect for others? What we teach—our attitudes to the world and our own engagement in the world—will have an influence on our students. How are we preparing our students to love their neighbors?

18. How much is learning in my classroom related to the world beyond?

God has created for us a world with unparalleled complexity, codependence, integration, and diversity. And yet all people are our neighbors (Luke 10:29–37), and this understanding should shape our response to the world. Do we offer opportunities for learning that place great value on seeing knowledge, our world, and our place within God's world in an integrated way under God's sovereign rule? Do we promote our students' understanding of their role as global citizens, and an understanding that God has plans for the future of his world?

How well do we deal with differences in race, religion, and culture within our classrooms? Do we project and encourage attitudes of acceptance toward others and an appreciation of difference? We must seek to help our students understand the diversity of the world and understand the key role they play within it as agents of God's grace. Our students must increasingly be prepared for life in the world as global citizens.

19. How important is narrative in your classroom and school?

As we discussed in chapter 7, people tell stories, learn from stories in their varied forms, and frequently share their lives with other students through stories. The Bible is filled with stories and it is a key way in which God communicates with us. God has given us the ability to tell stories and understand them as a key means of his revelation to us. It is through God's stories we understand who he is. As God's creatures made in his image, the stories we share directly and indirectly in life can point to or away from God. How do the stories we share at school suggest our views on the value of humanity, our beliefs, hopes, fears, and knowledge? Is my classroom a place where children tell their stories, and where others listen and gain hope and inspiration to seek God? To what extent are our stories and those we encourage in school life, echoes of the central meta-narrative of the Bible, God's redemptive plan for his people? For as Tolkien suggested, the gospel of Christ is "the greatest story of them all."[19]

20. Do our pedagogical practices demonstrate a relationship between education and discipleship?

God made us to be disciples and to make disciples (Matt 28:18–20; 2 Tim 2:2). The way we structure our classrooms and our activities should allow and promote opportunities for discipleship. The learning activities, texts, and forms of imitation we encourage are vehicles by which character

19. Ware, *God and the Fairy Tale*, 2.

and godly wisdom are developed and sustained. Are our classrooms and schools simply places of fierce individual achievement and competition, or places where all have the opportunity to learn from and teach others? As the Apostle Paul challenged the church in Rome, do we seek maturity in our students through the transformation and renewal of their minds (Rom 12:2)?

Do the things we say and the priorities we demonstrate show that we see our true citizenship as in heaven? Or is our pedagogy devoted to promoting the achievements and benefits of this world without regard for the next?

APPLICATION OF THE PEDAGOGICAL FRAMEWORK WITHIN THE SCHOOL AND CLASSROOM

On the pages that follow, I present four case studies. Each in its own way demonstrates varied dimensions of life in the classroom and school. They are designed to encourage discussion of common events in a school, and how the framework helps us discuss the way we might deal with each situation. As well, my hope is each case might help teachers to assess common situations within schools, and how we might identify authentic practices in response that place a priority upon the kingdom of God.

Case Study 1: "The Non-talking Group"

A number of years ago I was directing a research project concerning literacy. The project was an investigation of the early writing of children within a rural public school. I had approached the principal and negotiated access as a researcher to visit a Kindergarten class each week for a two-hour period. The purpose was to work with five-year-old children who had been at school for about two months, and had on the whole just started to acquire some early reading skills. They were also trying to master handwriting. They had been given very little opportunity to explore freewriting. The researcher working on the project entered the school on day one and gave the children blank books with a space for them to write their names. There was a label on the front cover that said "My Writing Book." The children were asked each week to write. Some were puzzled and wrote little, others drew, some wrote numbers and letters and a few wrote words. As the researcher moved around the room he would ask them what they had been writing, and most would talk intelligently about their "work." After a few weeks, the Head of Infants at the school visited the classroom due to her interest in the work. She had heard from some of the children and their teachers about the writing. She watched the researcher as he worked with the children. She came up later and spoke to him. She said she was impressed by what the children were doing. And then she said something that was surprising: "You know, that little girl who was just talking to you is in our non-talkers group." To which the researcher replied, "Who, Stephanie? She's a real chatterbox." "Might be," she replied, "but she hasn't said anything in class all year."

What does this Case Study Teach Us?

The case study illustrates a number of elements within the framework above. First, it demonstrates that one of the wonders of the way God created people is he made each of us as unique individuals who have worth in his sight (Principle 1). Some are quiet and some are outgoing. Getting to know our children well is important. Without this we are in no position to nurture their growth as learners and children of God. As teachers, we need to be able to see what is unique and precious in all children. The researcher was able to do this during one visit per week, while for the classroom teacher, the child was unknown. Of course, the classroom practices might have contributed to the child's new-found gift of talk. This demonstrates some of the complexity of teaching as we orchestrate learning activities, observe our children, and try to get to know them all at the same time. It also emphasizes why the use of varied methods is important (Principle 11).

The case study also provides an interesting insight into how a specific curriculum activity can provide opportunities for children to demonstrate some of their God-given qualities as learners. Stephanie responds well to a strategy that gives her more responsibility for her learning, and that offers opportunities for creativity and risk-taking (Principles 8, 9, 10, and 11). As well, the practice allowed the individual needs of the child to be met (Principle 7).

Case Study 2: "Parent-Teacher Night"

Parent-teacher nights are always a stressful time for teachers. How much information should be given to parents, and what focus should the information have? A school was trialing a new reporting format that offered numerical marks and grades for all school subjects, as well as a detailed checklist of behavioral items, several of which commented on the spiritual growth of the child. Karen found it hard to complete the final section because the parents of her children were not all Christians. In fact, she knew at least one father was an atheist, and that he wasn't too keen on the Christian education component of the curriculum. And yet, the parents' child had grown in a remarkable way throughout the year in relation to their knowledge of God and interest in Bible study. There were other children who had shown little interest in God, who had very committed Christian parents. Karen hated filling out this section of the report. Ultimately, she ended up using a number of stock phrases that weren't too offensive and didn't lead to many questions. Things like, "Billy has shown interest in Christian education classes," "Celeste enjoys learning about God," and so on. As a result, few parents wanted to ask about this section of the report and Karen managed to escape difficult conversations about the children's spiritual growth.

What does this Case Study Teach Us?

Karen is facing what is one of the most common and difficult challenges faced by the Christian teacher in the Christian school. While it is her desire to see all children come to faith, she knows most children in her care are unregenerate, and that some come from families that have done little to teach and nurture the Christian faith. So for Karen the challenge in introducing her class to Christ is in knowing how she can nurture them. She can obviously pray for all of her children and can teach the Bible faithfully at school and seek to be a godly example to her class, but can she do more?

If the child has had the foundations of faith laid like Paul's young disciple Timothy, then perhaps Karen's task is simply to continue the work done in the family. Second Timothy 3:10–17 demonstrates how both are important and are related. Paul commends Timothy for following "my teaching, my conduct, my aim in life, my faith, my patience, my love, my steadfastness, my persecutions and sufferings . . ." (vv. 10–11a). As well, he urges Timothy to continue in "what you have learned and have firmly believed, knowing from whom you learned it and how from childhood you have been acquainted with the sacred writings which are able to make you wise for salvation through faith in Christ Jesus" (2 Tim 3:14b–15). Here Paul shows how important the relationship is between the teaching of childhood and later teaching and discipleship. Of course, while the young Timothy was well prepared by his family, this cannot be assumed, even in the Christian families associated with our schools. For some children, the Christian school and the local church will be the major source of Christian teaching in their early years, whether in a school, Sunday school, youth group, Scripture in schools program[20], or an after-school club.

The key for Karen would seem to be to remember that it is only by the Spirit of God that wisdom is given. Paul reminded the Corinthian church it was not merely their words they taught that changed people, but the work of God through them. In ways that are difficult for us to grasp, the teacher is able to declare " ... God's wisdom, a mystery that has been hidden and that God destined for our glory before time began" (1 Cor 2:7). Karen is able to impart this wisdom "in words not taught by human wisdom but taught by the Spirit, interpreting spiritual truths to those who are spiritual" (1 Cor 2:13b). Just as the apostles taught in the presence of the believer and the non-believer, so too the teacher will be called to teach children who know Christ and others who do not. The Christian school offers the opportunity for the foundations of faith to be laid. This is in contrast to Timothy who first heard the teachings of Scripture at home, as would have been the case for other Jewish families, and indeed is the case for some of the students of Christian families today.

A challenge for Karen in this is the need to communicate honestly to the Christian and the non-Christian parent, and as she does so, to trust God will use her words according to his purposes. Once again, this case study demonstrates a number of the principles of the framework. We need to understand the foundations of Christian teaching in the homes of our children (Principle 2), and we cannot forget the important relationship between education and discipleship (Principle 20). Finally, we need to be honest in our dealings with students and parents. Everything we do should reflect a right view of the place our work as teachers has in God's redemptive work and in the honoring of his name (Principle 4).

---

20. International readers please note that under Australian law the church can offer up to sixty minutes of religious instruction each week in government-funded public schools.

Case Study 3: "Justice and Forgiveness"

Kelly was a grade six student who had just celebrated her twelfth birthday. The most exciting gift she received was a new iPhone. Not surprisingly, there was a little gadget envy among her classmates whose parents had varied attitudes toward phones and technology. At least half of the class had no prospect of a phone until high school, but several already had iPhones, and another group of about eight students had more modest phones. The school had a policy that phones were to be kept in bags and not taken out until students left the playground at the end of the day. But Kelly couldn't help herself and had been showing its features off during lunch, taking photos and watching a YouTube video clip of the band One Direction.

Kelly put the phone back in her bag after lunch, but when the day ended and she left school, she couldn't find it. She went back to school to look for it and noticed one of the boys from her class (Chris), disappearing in the opposite direction with one of his friends laughing as they went. She couldn't find the phone anywhere so she went home in a distraught state. That night she revealed the loss to her parents. They were frustrated that an expensive item had been lost, and they visited the school the next day to find out what might have happened.

The next morning Kelly's parents visited the class teacher and in turn the Principal. Later that day Kelly's teacher quizzed the class to see if anyone knew anything about Kelly's phone. Several said they'd been looking at it with her the previous lunchtime, but no one knew anything about its disappearance. The school promised to keep investigating and reminded the class about the school rules in relation to phones. That night at about 8:30 p.m. Kelly's mother received a phone call from the mother of Chris, who had mysteriously acquired an iPhone that she discovered while putting clothes away in his drawers. When confronted by his mother, he had confessed to taking it from Kelly's bag. Chris would take the phone back the next day and face whatever punishment the school decided it should hand out. Chris was grounded for a month, and told that the phone he was going to receive for his 12th birthday wouldn't be bought until at least his thirteenth birthday.

The next day at school Chris had to confront Kelly and apologize, visit the principal's office to hear about a one week immediate suspension, and be ostracized by anyone who saw him, for the word had got around concerning his stupidity and dishonesty. In the week that followed, Kelly's teacher had a number of occasions that required her to comment on the iPhone saga. These included intervening in a heated conversation between Kelly's and Chris's friends about the punishment he received, talking about the need to be careful when bringing special belongings to school, and the reason for rules such as "no phones out of bags." It seemed that some were quick to take sides and try to either make excuses for Chris or feel outraged on behalf of Kelly.

What does this Case Study Teach Us?

This scenario is typical of many in schools. Every day teachers are required to administer justice. There will always be punishment to be handed out for inappropriate behavior. As well, there will be many people impacted by the events, in addition to the many who will react to them. For each of these instances in the life of the classroom, there will be numerous opportunities for growth and learning. How the teacher and the school deals with matters of this kind are opportunities to enact fair responses, hand out just punishments, and ensure that students are encouraged to show forgiveness and understanding, not vilification and judgment. The teacher and principal in this case needed to show great wisdom in how they acted. There were many parties to consider. First, there was Chris, who needed to be reminded of his wrong action, punished for it, and encouraged to consider what he needed to do in response. Second, his parents needed to respond appropriately by helping their child understand why his actions were wrong without making excuses for him. Third, Kelly's parents needed to deal with the loss of a material object, keep this in right perspective, and ensure that Kelly examined her actions to make sure she understood that as well as breaking school rules, she had contributed to the temptation and envy that Chris experienced. And finally, the friends of Kelly and Chris needed to understand their own reactions, consider their responses, and demonstrate patience and forgiveness towards Chris.

Once again, there are many opportunities for varied principles within the pedagogical framework to be demonstrated. The teacher, parents, and principal all needed to remember that punishment and discipline are part of good pedagogy (Principle 14). They also needed to seek and model justice within the school and classroom (Principle 17), and that in situations like this we are to seek repentance while showing forgiveness and strengthening the life of the community and shared practices and beliefs (Principle 14). This case study illustrates that in the simple events of classroom life, how justice, forgiveness, and punishment are reconciled and enacted matters greatly.

Case Study 4: "Recognizing Creativity and Difference"

This case study concerns one teacher's experience of two parents who had expressed strong views on the type of books that were being used and recommended in her grade five classroom. Kathy was an enthusiastic teacher in a Christian school. About 60 percent of the children in her class were from Christian families. She was a keen teacher of reading and literacy, and had several strands to her program. She read quality literature to her class on a daily basis, to which varied responses were invited. Sometimes no set response activities were requested, but on other occasions students responded through writing (e.g., a reading journal, character descriptions, drawing, readers' theatre, and so on), discussion, drama, and so on. All students had a time of independent reading each day, and she had a comprehension strand with varied texts and activities that were done three times a week.

In about week six of term one, the father of a student named Emily requested an appointment to discuss the literature she was reading at school. Emily's father was a small business owner and saw the importance of literacy for work and life. He was also a Christian and was keen for Emily to have both a strong reading program at school, and books that he saw as suitable. When he met with the teacher he thanked her for her enthusiasm and professionalism, but indicated that he was unhappy about the choice of literature she was reading to them, as well as the books she was recommending to Emily. His concern was the teacher seemed to read lots of fantasy, and that Emily was increasingly reading this same genre at home. He cited *Playing Beatie Bow*[21] by Ruth Park as unsuitable.

The teacher had just read the well-known Australian novel for young adolescents to the class. It is essentially a time-slip story in which a young girl is taken back in time to Sydney in 1873. After watching children in the streets playing an old ghost game called "Beatie Bow," the main character Abigail finds herself chasing a strange-looking girl. Abigail travels up and down narrow lanes and streets and ends up in a household where one family member has the gift of seeing into and visiting the future. The father felt that the emphasis on superstition and ghosts was inappropriate

---

21. Park, *Playing Beatie Bow*.

in a Christian school. He also expressed concern at J. R. R. Tolkien's *The Hobbit*[22] and the 1963 Newbery Medal–winning science fiction fantasy *A Wrinkle in Time*,[23] by Madeleine L'Engle. Emily's father suggested that too much fantasy and science fiction was not helpful for young children, as it was confusing and in conflict with biblical teaching. He also suggested that fantasy was potentially damaging to their faith.

In the third week of term two a second parent requested a meeting to discuss the type of books that were being shared in literature. The mother, Karen, was a lawyer but was not a Christian. Her main concern was she didn't want her daughter Shannon to be subjected to books with stereotypical female role models, citing older classic books as the major culprits. She cited *The Lord of the Rings*[24] as lacking strong female characters, and the reading of a book of Shakespearean stories,[25] adapted by the great English writer Leon Garfield, as particularly inappropriate and lacking any strong female role models. She felt the teacher should be promoting books that have stronger girls or women, and that contemporary literature was more appropriate for children today. She also suggested that the common role of 'hero" as the strong white male was too common in older books. Her view was the world was always seen in such stories as controlled and made by men, heroes who shape the world, rescuing women from disaster and generally making the world a better place. She commented, "where are women in this? Just passengers, being saved by strong men!" She also cited a unit on Greek myths as being particularly dominated by the heroic theme, and again suggested that much more contemporary fiction would help to overcome these negative and stereotypical portrayals.

What does this Case Study Teach Us?

I guess, to start with, it shows why it's so hard to be a teacher! It also shows that parents can have many different opinions about things as basic as what is good literature. The teacher has to deal with one parent who is reacting primarily based on ideological grounds, and a second who is challenging what is appropriate literature for someone who has a Christian worldview. The difficulty is both parents raise legitimate points. There is a need to

22. Tolkien, *The Hobbit*.
23. L'Engle, *A Wrinkle in Time*.
24. Tolkien, *The Lord of the Rings*.
25. Garfield, *Shakespeare Stories*.

present varied literature, and to ensure boys and girls have the opportunity to read books that offer positive models. They do need to read books that explore fully what it means to be human, as well as to be female and male, of different races and religion, and so on. But both parents seem to fail to understand that education is not simply about training children's minds, and if it was, feeding them a restricted diet of books that match the parents' idea of an appropriate worldview might not work anyway. There are also competing notions here about what makes literature good.

The first parent fails to recognize that fantasy is vital for the stimulation of children's imaginations (Principle 9). God made us to be imaginative and creative beings. In fact, as I have already outlined at length, it is at least partly through our imaginations and longings that we seek him and experience all he intended for us. The second parent misses another vital point. It is only by engaging with varied texts and people that communicate different views of the world that we can adequately discover what we believe about human potential, roles, and even gendered stereotypes. This is what I mean by "creative risk-taking and problem-solving" in the framework above (Principle 10). Both parents also make the mistake of indirectly promoting a view of literature that is rather homogenized. Anthony Esolen talks about this error in his book *Ten Ways to Destroy the Imagination of Your Child*.[26] He argues that when you remove fantasy and replace it with real life and contemporary literature, "you drown the stories, or you flatten them into homogeneity . . . you turn all stories into a bald, brazen sales pitch, preferably a political pitch."

If we do as these two parents wish, we in effect fail to help our students learn from the stories of the past and grapple with people, relationships, and even role models that are not as they seem in the present age. Esolen paraphrases Emily Dickinson, who commented on the power of literature to transform. Essentially, reading is not about us; rather, it offers a journey "to lands unknown,"[27] places where we can learn new things and even see our own situations in new ways.[28]

The second parent, Karen, who was so strongly against heroes and saviors and was seeking stronger female role models for her daughter, was confusing the purpose of literature. While I share her concern for more books with women who achieve in all walks of life, I believe she makes a

26. Esolen, *Ten Ways to Destroy the Imagination*, 99.

27. Ibid., 105.

28. Cairney, *Other Worlds*.

serious mistake when she fails to understand her daughter can learn much that is inspirational in both the men and women in the very books she criticizes. For stories are not recipes for human stereotypes, but a journey into the lives of others. As well, there can be no more important human quality than to show strength of character and to conquer adversity and evil. There is much that her daughter Shannon could learn in the stories of Tolkien, Shakespeare, and the myths of ancient Greece. The hero (or the heroine) is so foundational to the finest of human virtues, that to deny it is simply to want to create a world in which all are equally meritorious and capable of all things, whether courage, compassion, or academic excellence. God made us all in his image as creatures capable of different roles and actions (Principle 1). We are to grow in humility as creatures who learn from one another (Principle 6). As well, the case study highlights the need to constantly evaluate the ends towards which our pedagogy is directed (Principle 13). Lifelong discipleship encourages our students to examine their own lives, and to consider the practices they engage in and whether that are helpful for the good (Principles 19 and 20).

DRAWING IT ALL TOGETHER

I believe any school or community undergirded by the Christian faith will be different. A Christian classroom is one in which the teacher deftly orchestrates classroom life in such a way that she and her students will increasingly demonstrate lives that are attentive to other members of a community. We don't just absorb knowledge or even the experience of others. Rather, in our state of "wonderful difference," each member of a class or school community is a gift to those around them. Learning will flourish in classrooms where Christian teachers demonstrate deep engagement with students, as well as active reflection on their actions, language, goals, and desires. Such teachers will be responsive and alert to differences, and will demonstrate a love for their students and teaching. Learning is not the static individual reception of knowledge and perfect understanding. Rather, it is immersion in a life that is only partly lived at school. As we have discussed in this book, our students have complex lives in which they dwell as part of numerous communities of practice. Our students engage with others who are fellow knowledge-bearers and meaning-makers. Life and learning involve engagement with a vast array of other people as we share each other's stories, hunches, new ideas, knowledge, and experience. Learning is always enacted in some way and embedded within varied communities of practice. Collectively, in any classroom or school, our varied experiences of learning provide us with opportunities to demonstrate achievements and failures, courageous attempts, and acts reflective of the full array of human qualities. Our students learn from others, and are shaped by life at school. When their teachers sees the formation of students for the kingdom of God as their priority, we can be confident God is at work in the school.

I am reminded of French Christian philosopher Paul Ricoeur and his work on the "metaphorical imagination." Ricoeur contended that a fulfilled person takes seriously their teleology—that is, their apparent purpose, directions, and goals in life. Our teleology both reflects and helps shape our hopes and dreams, as we live our lives in all of its fullness.[29] This life of course includes our relationships, our education, our immersion in varied cultural practices, and our many experiences of the world. This is a world filled with varied communities of practice, relationships, and stories, where we imagine and think our way along life's path as we seek possibilities for our future.

Ricoeur suggested "authentic faith emerges by way of its circuitous travels through a sustained hermeneutics of suspicion."[30] As we go through this life, our presuppositions are challenged daily as we seek to understand our life experiences. He suggested that the "metaphorical imagination" is implicated in our articulation and understanding of faith, and in fact "is an ally for the understanding and articulation of faith."[31] The imagination, in effect, enables us to "generate new metaphors for synthesizing disparate aspects of reality" that challenge our assumptions.[32] All of life has an impact on us, including reading that can "disclose new possibilities . . . and expanded views of the world and a deeper capacity for selfhood."[33] In essence, Ricoeur was contending that just as religious texts such as the Bible can be revelatory, so too can literature—not as inspired truth—but because it is able to prime a union between one's experience of the world and the "revelation" of texts. In effect, the aesthetic can help to provide access to the sacred.[34] Ricoeur argued we can experience "redemption through imagina-

29. Ricoeur, *Figuring the Sacred*, loc. 120, para. 1, line 3.

30. Ibid., loc. 127, para. 1.

31. Ibid., loc 131, para. 2, lines 2–4.

32. Ibid., loc 135, para. 1, lines 6–8.

33. Ibid., loc 138, para. 2, lines 1–4.

34. Ibid., loc. 150.

tion," because in "imagining his possibilities, man can act as a prophet of his own experience."[35]

In essence, I have contended in this book that all of life can be used by God as he reveals himself to us. The things we teach, the priorities we set, the activities we plan, the experiences that are structured, the books we share; indeed, all of life in and outside the school acts upon us and shapes us. Christian schools seek to structure curriculum and learning to satisfy the education of the child. This is an education in knowledge and skills which is important. But above all else, Christian schools exist to reveal God in every aspect of the life of the classroom and school. Pedagogy is the vehicle for shaping the life of the school to point our students toward Christ.

FORMATION: EDUCATING FOR CHARACTER AND FAITH

Throughout this book, I have spoken much about formation. I have argued that the chief task of the Christian school is the formation of its students. Some have used the softer term "character" to suggest similar life goals, but my preference is "formation," for it suggests the action of forming or the process of being formed, whereas "character" refers to the mental and moral qualities distinctive to the individual. When coupled with "education" to become "education of character," then of course action is also implied. Without action, we run the risk of seeing faith as simply about transmitting ideas.

The Christian school is to be one that is in the business of shaping young lives for the good. As Martin Buber says in the quote, written in 1947, that headed this final chapter,

> Education worthy of its name is essentially education of character. For the genuine educator does not merely consider individual functions of his pupils, as one intending to teach him only to know or be capable of certain things; but his concern is always the person as a whole, both in the actuality in which he lives before you now and in the possibilities, what he can become.[36]

Buber suggested that the teacher, in effect, presents a selection of the world to his or her students with the formation of character as the key central purpose. These forces within the teacher, he contends, are "eternally

35. Ricoeur, *Image of God*, 127.
36. Buber, *Between Man and Man*, 123.

the same: they are the world bound up in community, turned to God. The educator himself [sic] to be their vehicle."[37]

The task and calling of the teacher is indeed an honorable one. What could be a greater privilege than to have responsibility for the shaping of the hearts and minds of children? To be vehicles for learning and the revelation of God through his word and the witness of his people. This is a work that has eternal significance and is a privileged responsibility. We surely need God's enabling for such a task, and we need to cling to and trust in him as we embark down this path. I conclude with the following words from Paul and trust that they might be an encouragement for the task ahead.

> Finally, brothers and sisters, whatever is true, whatever is noble, whatever is right, whatever is pure, whatever is lovely, whatever is admirable—if anything is excellent or praiseworthy—think about such things. Whatever you have learned or received or heard from me, or seen in me—put it into practice. And the God of peace will be with you. (Phil 4:8–9)

37. Ibid., 106.

Bibliography

Anderson, Lorin W., and David R. Krathwohl, eds. *A Taxonomy for Learning, Teaching, and Assessing: A Revision of Bloom's Taxonomy of Educational Objectives.* Complete ed. New York: Longman, 2002.

Atwell, Nancie. *In the Middle: New Understandings about Writing, Reading, and Learning.* 2nd ed. Portsmouth, NH: Boynton/Cook, 1998.

Augustine. *Augustine: Later Works.* Translated by John Burnaby. Philadelphia: Westminster, 1955.

Banks, Daniel. "Hip Hop as Pedagogy: Something from Something." *Theatre Topics* 25 (2015) 243–59.

Barnes, Douglas. *From Communication to Curriculum.* Harmondsworth, UK: Penguin, 1976.

Barr, James. *The Semantics of Biblical Language.* London: Oxford University Press, 1961.

Beech, Geoff. *Christians as Teachers: What Might it Look Like?* Eugene, OR: Wipf & Stock, 2015.

Blomberg, Doug. *Wisdom and Curriculum: Christian Schooling after Modernity.* Sioux Center, IA: Dordt College Press, 2007.

Blyton, Enid. *The Enchanted Wood.* London: Newnes, 1939.

Bourdieu, Pierre. *Distinction: A Social Critique of the Judgment of Taste.* Translated by Richard Nice. Cambridge, MA: Harvard University Press, 1984.

———. *The Logic of Practice.* Translated by Richard Nice. Stanford: Stanford University Press, 1990.

———. *Outline of a Theory of Practice.* Translated by Richard Nice. Cambridge: Cambridge University Press, 1977.

Brown, John Seely, et al. "Situated Cognition and the Culture of Learning." *Educational Researcher* 18 (1989) 32–42.

Brueggemann, Walter. *The Creative Word: Canon as a Model for Biblical Education.* Philadelphia: Fortress, 1982.

Bruner, Jerome. *Actual Minds, Possible Worlds.* Cambridge, MA: Harvard University Press, 1986.

———. *Child's Talk: Learning to Use Language.* Oxford: Oxford University Press, 1983.

Buber, Martin. *Between Man and Man.* Translated by Ronald Gregor Smith. London: Routledge & Kegan Paul, 1965.

Bunyan, John. *Dangerous Journey: The Story of Pilgrim's Progress.* Abridged by Oliver Hunkin. Grand Rapids: Eerdmans, 1985.

Cairney, Trevor H. "Beyond the Classroom Walls: The Discovery of the Family and Community as Partners in Education." *Educational Review* 52 (2000) 163–74.

―――. "Community Literacy Practices and Education: Australia." In *Encyclopaedia of Language and Education*, edited by Brian Street, 207–25. 3rd ed. London: Kluwer Academic, 2017.

―――. "Intertextuality: Infectious Echoes from the Past." *The Reading Teacher* 43 (1990) 478–84.

―――. "Literacy Diversity: Understanding and Responding to the Textual Tapestries of Home, School and Community." In *Portraits of Literacy Across Families, Communities, and Schools: Intersections and Tensions*, edited by Jim Anderson et al., 41–61. Mahwah, NJ: L. Erlbaum Associates, 2005.

―――. *Other Worlds: The Endless Possibilities of Literature.* Portsmouth, NH: Heinemann, 1990.

―――. *Pathways to Literacy.* London: Cassell, 1995.

―――. "The Social Foundations of Literacy." *Australian Journal of Reading* 10 (1987) 84–96.

―――. "Storytelling and Life: The Place of Stories in Christian Formation." *Case Quarterly* 30 (2012) 3–8.

―――. "Supporting the Independent Learners: Negotiating Change in the Classroom." In *Independent Learners at School*, edited by Joelie Hancock and Barbara Comber, 78–96. North Ryde, Australia: Methuen, 1987.

―――. *Teaching Reading Comprehension: Meaning Makers at Work.* Milton Keynes, UK: Open University Press, 1990.

Cairney, Trevor H., and Jean Ashton. "Three Families, Multiple Discourses: Parental Roles, Constructions of Literacy and Diversity of Pedagogic Practice." *Linguistics in Education* 13 (2002) 303–45.

Cairney, Trevor H., et al. *New Perspectives in Anglican Education: Reconsidering Purpose and Plotting a Future Direction.* Sydney: Anglican Education Commission, 2011.

Cairney, Trevor H., and Lynne Munsie. *Beyond Tokenism: Parents as Partners in Literacy.* Portsmouth, NH: Heinemann, 1995.

Cairney, Trevor H., and Jenny Ruge. *Community Literacy Practices and Schooling: Towards Effective Support for Students.* Canberra, Australia: Department of Employment, Education, and Training, 1998.

Cairney, Trevor H., and David Starling, eds. *Theology and the Future: Evangelical Assertions and Explorations.* London: T. & T. Clark, 2014.

Calvin, John. *Institutes of the Christian Religion.* Edited by John T. McNeill. Translated by Ford Lewis Battles. 2 vols. Atlanta: John Knox, 1975.

Chalmers, Thomas. "The Expulsive Power of a New Affection." https://redeemerchurch. files.wordpress.com/2013/01/expulsive-power-of-a-great-affection.pdf.

Collier, John. "Models of Christian Education." *TEACH Journal of Christian Education* 7 (2013) 4–7. http://research.avondale.edu.au/teach/vol7/iss1/2/.

Cooling, Trevor, et al. *Christian Faith in English Church Schools.* Oxford: P. Lang, 2016.

Cowling, Brian. "The Context of Anglican Education." In *New Perspectives in Anglican Education: Reconsidering Purpose and Plotting a Future Direction*, by Trevor H. Cairney et al., 25–40. Sydney: Anglican Education Commission, 2011.

De Graaff, Arnold H., and Jean Olthuis, eds. *Joy in Learning: An Integrated Curriculum for the Elementary School.* Vol. 1. Toronto: Curriculum Development Centre, 1973.

Dykstra, Craig. *Growing in the Life of Faith: Education and Christian Practices.* Louisville: Geneva, 1999.

Dykstra, Craig, and Dorothy C. Bass. "A Theological Understanding of Christian Practices." *Lifelong Faith* (Summer 2008) 3–13. http://www.faithformation2020.net/uploads/5/1/6/4/5164069/theological_understanding_of_practice_-_bass.pdf.

———. "Times of Yearning, Practices of Faith." In *Practicing Our Faith: A Way of Life for a Searching People*, edited by Dorothy C. Bass, 1–12. 2nd ed. San Francisco: J. Wiley, 2010.

Esolen, Anthony. *Ten Ways to Destroy the Imagination of Your Child*. Wilmington, DE: ISI, 2010.

Estes, Daniel J. *Hear, My Son: Teaching and Learning in Proverbs 1–9*. Downers Grove, IL: InterVarsity, 2003.

Farley, Edward. *Ecclesial Man: A Social Phenomenology of Faith and Reality*. Philadelphia: Fortress, 1975.

Fernie, David, et al. "Becoming a Person in the Preschool: Creating Integrated Gender, School Culture, and Peer Culture Positioning." *International Journal of Qualitative Studies in Education* 6 (1993) 95–110.

Frame, John. "Presuppositional Apologetics." In *Five Views on Apologetics*, edited by Steven B. Cowan and Stanley N. Gundry, 208–31. Grand Rapids: Zondervan, 2000.

Freire, Paulo. *Pedagogy of the Oppressed*. Translated by Myra Bergman Ramos. New York: Seabury, 1970.

Friedman, Maurice. "Introduction." In *Between Man and Man*, by Martin Buber. Translated by Ronald Gregor-Smith. London: Routledge & Keegan, 1947.

Garfield, Leon. *Shakespeare Stories*. New York: Houghton Mifflin, 1985.

Gee, James Paul. *Social Linguistics and Literacies: Ideology in Discourses*. 2nd ed. London: Taylor & Francis, 1996.

Goodlet, Ken, and John Collier, eds. *Teaching Well: Insights for Educators in Christian Schools*. Sydney: Barton, 2014.

Gunton, Colin E. "Knowledge and Culture: Towards an Epistemology of the Concrete." In *Gospel and Contemporary Culture*, edited by Hugh Montefiore, 84–102. London: Mowbray, 1992.

Gurley, Jennifer. "Platonic *Paideia*." *Philosophy and Literature* 23 (1999) 351–77.

Gutierrez, Kris D. "How Talk, Context and Script Shape Contexts for Learning: A Cross-Case Comparison of Journal Sharing." *Linguistics and Education* 5:3–4 (1993) 335–65.

Harste, Jerome C., et al. *Language Stories and Literacy Lessons*. Portsmouth, NH: Heinemann Educational, 1984.

Hart, Trevor. *Between the Image and the Word: Theological Engagements with Imagination*. Farnham, UK: Ashgate, 2013.

———. "Givenness, Grace and Gratitude: Creation, Artistry and Eucharist." New College Lectures. New College, University of New South Wales, New Zealand. September 4, 2008. http://www.ncv.unsw.edu.au/audios/audio-archives.

Hauerwas, Stanley. *Hannah's Child: A Theologian's Memoir*. Grand Rapids: Eerdmans, 2010.

———. *The State of the University: Academic Knowledges and the Knowledge of God*. Malden, MA: Blackwell, 2007.

———. "A Story-Formed Community: Reflections on *Watership Down*." In *The Hauerwas Reader*, edited by John Berkman and Michael Cartwright, 171–99. Durham, NC: Duke University Press, 2001.

Hays, Richard B. *The Conversion of the Imagination: Paul as Interpreter of Israel's Scripture.* Grand Rapids: Eerdmans, 2005.

Heap, James. "What Counts as Reading: Limits to Certainty in Assessment." *Curriculum Inquiry* 10 (1980) 265–92.

Heras, Ana Inés. "The Construction of Understanding in a Sixth-Grade Classroom." *Linguistics and Education* 5 (1993) 275–99.

Higton, Mike. *A Theology of Higher Education.* Oxford: Oxford University Press, 2012.

Hodgson, Peter C. *God's Wisdom: Toward a Theology of Education.* Louisville: Westminster John Knox, 1999.

Hohne, David. "Becoming an Apologetic Person." *Case* 20 (2009) 4–9.

Holmes, Arthur A. *Building the Christian Academy.* Grand Rapids: Eerdmans, 2001.

Hull, John. "Aiming for Christian Education, Settling for Christians Educating: The Christian School's Replication of a Public School Paradigm." *Christian Scholar Review* 32 (2009) 203–23.

Hyman, R. T. *Strategic Questioning.* Englewood Cliffs, NJ: Prentice-Hall, 1979.

Jeffreys, M. V. C. *Glaucon: An Inquiry into the Aims of Education.* London: Pitman, 1950.

Jensen, Michael. "The Creature Who Learns: A Theological Anthropology for Christian Education." In *New Perspectives in Anglican Education: Reconsidering Purpose and Plotting a Future Direction,* by Trevor H. Cairney et al., 41–57. Sydney: Anglican Education Commission, 2011.

Kearney, Richard. *Poetics of Imagining: Modern to Postmodern.* Edinburgh: Edinburgh University Press, 1998.

Keller, Tim. *The Reason for God: Belief in an Age of Skepticism.* New York: Dutton, 2008.

Ladson-Billings, Gloria. *The Dreamkeepers: Successful Teachers of African American Children.* 2nd ed. San Francisco: Jossey-Bass, 2009.

Lave, Jean, and Etienne Wenger. *Situated Learning: Legitimate Peripheral Participation.* Cambridge: University of Cambridge Press, 1991.

L'Engle, Madeleine. *A Wrinkle in Time.* New York: Farrar, Straus and Giroux, 1963.

Lewis, C. S. "Bluspels and Flalansferes: A Semantic Nightmare." In *Rehabilitations and Other Essays,* 56–77. London: Oxford University Press, 1939.

Little, Sara. "Theology and Education." In *Harper's Encyclopaedia of Religious Education,* edited by Iris V. Cully and Kendig Brubaker Cully, 649–51. San Francisco: Harper & Row, 1990.

Louden, William, et al. *In Teachers' Hands: Effective Literacy Teaching Practices in the Early Years of Schooling.* Perth: Edith Cowan University, 2005.

MacIntyre, Alasdair. *After Virtue: A Study in Moral Theory.* 2nd ed. Notre Dame, IN: University of Notre Dame Press, 1984.

———. *Three Rival Versions of Moral Enquiry: Encyclopaedia, Genealogy, and Tradition.* 7th ed. Notre Dame, IN: University of Notre Dame Press, 2012.

MacIntyre, Alasdair, and Joseph Dunne. "Alasdair MacIntyre on Education: In Dialogue with Joseph Dunne." *Journal of Philosophy of Education* 36 (2002) 1–19.

McDowell, John. "The Future of Theology, or, Theological Education Beyond the Myth of the Secular." *Case Quarterly* 28 (2011) 16–21.

Meland, Bernard Eugene. *Higher Education and the Human Spirit.* Chicago: University of Chicago Press, 1953.

Neill, Alexander Sutherland. *Summerhill School: A New View of Childhood.* Edited by Albert Lamb. New York: Penguin, 1995.

O'Donovan, Oliver. *Common Objects of Love: Moral Reflection and the Shaping of Community*. Grand Rapids: Eerdman, 2002.

———. *Resurrection and Moral Order: An Outline for Evangelical Ethics*. London: Routledge, 2002.

Owocki, Gretchen, and Yetta Goodman. *Kidwatching: Documenting Children's Literacy Development*. Portsmouth, NH: Heinemann, 2002.

Park, Ruth. *Playing Beatie Bow*. Melbourne: Thomas Nelson, 1980.

Pazmino, Robert W. *Foundational Issues in Christian Education: An Introduction in Evangelical Perspective*. 3rd ed. Grand Rapids: Baker Academic, 2008.

Pietsch, James. "Classroom Culture and Relational Spaces." *Case Quarterly* 31 (2012) 15–19.

Polanyi, Michael. *Personal Knowledge: Towards a Post-critical Philosophy*. London: Routledge & Kegan Paul, 1958.

Reece, James H. *Lester and Clyde*. Gosford, Australia: Ashton Scholastic, 1976.

Ricoeur, Paul. *Figuring the Sacred: Religion, Narrative, and Imagination*. Translated by David Pellauer. Edited by Mark I. Wallace. Minneapolis: Fortress, 1995.

———. "The Image of God and the Epic of Man." In *History and Truth*, translated by Charles A. Kelbley, 110–28. Evanston, IL: Northwestern University Press, 1965.

Rogoff, Barbara. *Apprenticeship in Thinking: Cognitive Development in Social Context*. Cambridge, MA: Harvard University Press, 1991.

Rosen, Harold. *Stories and Meanings*. London: National Association for Teaching of English, 1986.

Rumelhart, David E. "Schemata: The Building Blocks of Cognition." In *Theoretical Issues in Reading Comprehension*, edited by Rand J. Spiro et al., 33–58. Hillsdale, NJ: L. Erlbaum Associates, 1984.

Scarratt, Dani. "Unearthing the Presuppositions of Presuppositionalism." http://www.case.edu.au/images/uploads/03_pdfs/scarratt-presuppositionalism.pdf.

Seuss, Dr. *There's a Wocket in My Pocket*. New York: Random House, 1974.

Smith, Bruce. "Hope and Tragedy in Life and Literature." *Case Quarterly* 30 (2012) 9–14.

Smith, Christian. *Moral, Believing Animals: Human Personhood and Culture*. New York: Oxford University Press, 2003.

Smith, Claire. "An Exploration of Early Christian Communities as 'Scholastic Communities' through a Study of the Vocabulary of 'Teaching' in 1 Corinthians, 1 and 2 Timothy and Titus." PhD diss., University of Western Sydney/Moore College, 2009.

Smith, David I., and James K. A. Smith. *Teaching and Christian Practices: Reshaping Faith and Learning*. Grand Rapids: Eerdmans, 2011.

Smith, James K. A. *Desiring the Kingdom: Worship, Worldview and Cultural Formation*. Grand Rapids: Baker Academic, 2009.

———. "Educating the Imagination: Christian Education as a Pedagogy of Desire." Plenary address to the "Education as Formation" conference, New College, University of New South Wales, Sydney, May 26, 2012. https://www.case.edu.au/blogs/case-subscription-library/educating-the-imagination-christian-education-as-a-pedagogy-of-desire.

———. "Educating the Imagination: Christian Education as a Pedagogy of Desire." *Case* 31 (2012) 9–14.

———. "Erotic Comprehension: The Bodily Basis of Meaning." New College Lectures, May 23, 2012, http://www.ncv.unsw.edu.au/audios/audio-archives.

Bibliography

———. "Imagining the Kingdom: On Christian Discipleship and Action." Unpublished manuscript, Lecture 1, New College Lectures, Sydney, May 23, 2012. http://www.newcollege.unsw.edu.au/audios/audio-archives.

———. "Sanctified Perception: How Worship Works." Unpublished lecture, New College Lectures, Sydney, May 24, 2012.

Sparrow, Tom, and Adam Hutchinson. *A History of Habit: From Aristotle to Bourdieu.* Lanham, MD: Lexington, 2013.

Speed, Diane. "What Might have Been: Creation and Eternity in Tolkien." *Case* 4 (2004) 12–13.

Starling, David I. *Uncorinthian Leadership.* Eugene, OR: Cascade, 2014.

Swann, Chris. "Humanising the Monster." *Case Quarterly* 30 (2012) 15–18.

Tanner, Kathryn. *Theories of Culture: A New Agenda for Theology.* Minneapolis: Fortress, 1997.

Tate, William. "Karl Barth's Secular Parables." *Case Quarterly* 30 (2012) 22–26.

Taylor, Charles. *Modern Social Imaginaries.* Durham, NC: Duke University Press, 2004.

Thiessen, Elmer J. *Teaching for Commitment: Liberal Education, Indoctrination & Christian Nurture.* Montreal: McGill-Queens University Press, 1993.

Tolkien, J. R. R. *The Hobbit.* New York: Spark, 2014.

———. *The Lord of the Rings.* New York: Ballantine, 1965.

———. *Tree and Leaf.* London: HarperCollins, 2001.

Tozer, A. W. *The Pursuit of God.* Harrisburg, PA: Christian Publications, 1948.

Urry, John. *The Tourist Gaze.* London: Sage, 1990.

Vanhoozer, Kevin J. "What is Everyday Theology? How and Why Christians Should Read Culture." In *Everyday Theology: How to Read Cultural Texts and Interpret Trends,* edited by Kevin J. Vanhoozer etal., 15–60. Grand Rapids: Baker Academic, 2007.

Veith, Gene Edward, Jr., and Matthew P. Ristuccia. *Imagination Redeemed: Glorifying God with a Neglected Part of Your Mind.* Wheaton, IL: Crossway, 2014.

Vygotsky, Lev S. *Mind in Society: The Development of Higher Psychological Processes.* Edited by Michael Cole, et al. Cambridge, MA: Harvard University Press, 1978.

———. "Thinking and Speech." In *The Collected Works of L. S. Vygotsky: Problems of General Psychology,* edited by Robert W. Rieber and Aaron S. Carton, 1:237–85. New York: Plenum, 1987.

Ware, Jim. *God and the Fairy Tale: Finding Truth in the Land of Make-Believe.* Colorado Springs, CO: Shaw, 2003.

Weick, Karl Edward. "Cognitive Processes in Organization." In *Research in Organizational Behavior,* edited by B. M. Staw, 1:41–74. Greenwich, CT: JAI Press, 1979.

Weiner, Irving B., ed. *Handbook of Psychology: Educational Psychology.* Vol. 7. 2nd ed. Hoboken, NJ: J. Wiley, 2003.

Wenger, Etienne. *Communities of Practice: Learning, Meaning, and Identity.* Cambridge: Cambridge University Press, 1998.

White, E. B. *Charlotte's Web.* New York: HarperCollins, 1952.

Williams, Rowan. *Grace and Necessity: Reflections on Art and Love.* Harrisburg, PA: Morehouse, 2005.

Wolterstorff, Nicholas. *Educating for Shalom: Essays on Christian Higher Education.* Edited by Clarence W. Joldersma and Gloria Goris Stronks. Grand Rapids: Eerdmans, 2004.

Wright, N.T. "The Bible and Christian Imagination." Lecture presented at Seattle Pacific University, May 18, 2005. *Response* 28.2 (2005). https://spu.edu/depts/uc/response/summer2k5/features/imagination.asp.

Index of Names and Subjects

Index of Scripture